PRONGHORN

PRONGHORN

Portrait of the
American Antelope

by GARY TURBAK

photographs by ALAN *and* SANDY CAREY

Northland Publishing

To my father, Melvin Turbak,
who first took me antelope hunting.

The author would like to thank the following people and agencies for their assistance with this book:
Bart O'Gara; Jim Yoakum; the Wildlife Management Institute; the Texas Parks and Wildlife Department;
the South Dakota Department of Game, Fish and Parks; the New Mexico Department of Game and Fish;
the Arizona Department of Game and Fish; the Montana Department of Fish, Wildlife, and Parks; and the
Nebraska Game and Parks Commission. A special thanks to Jim Yoakum for reviewing my manuscript.

Cover photo: Pronghorn buck, western Montana
Inset: Pronghorn buck, National Bison Range, Montana
Frontispiece: Pronghorn herd at sunset, Colorado (Robert Winslow)

The display type was set in Schneidler
The text type was set in Bulmer
Designed by Rudy J. Ramos
Edited by Karla Olson and Kathryn Wilder
Production supervised by Lisa Brownfield

Manufactured in Hong Kong by Sing Cheong

Copyright © 1995 by Gary Turbak
Photographs copyright © 1995 by Alan and Sandy Carey
All rights reserved.

This book may not be reproduced in whole or in part, by any means (with the exception of short quotes for the purpose of review),
without permission of the publisher. For information, address Northland Publishing Company, P. O. Box 1389, Flagstaff, Arizona 86002-1389.

All photographs are by Alan and Sandy Carey unless otherwise noted.
The publisher wishes to thank the following: Robert Campbell (pp. 22, 96, 104); Lee Kline (pp. 10, 33, 52, 61, 129, back cover);
Bob Miles/*Arizona Game and Fish* (pp. 118); James Tallon (pp. 97, 106, 124); Robert Winslow (pp. ii, viii, 30 68, 100, 112, 121, 130)

FIRST EDITION
ISBN 0-87358-595-X

Library of Congress Catalog Card Number 95-6508
Cataloging-in Publication Data
Turbak, Gary.
Pronghorn : portrait of the American antelope / by Gary Turbak ;
photographs by Alan and Sandy Carey. — 1st ed.
p.   cm.
Includes bibliographical references and index.
ISBN 0-87358-595-X : $15.95
1. Pronghorn antelope. I. Title.
QL737. U52T87 1995
599.73'58—dc20   95-6508

0495/7.5M/6-95

Contents

I'll Take the Prairie

IT IS EARLY OCTOBER in Montana. A hundred miles short of my hunting area, I start to spot pronghorns along the highway, and the fever in my soul boils a few degrees hotter. The antelope are why I'm here, and I'd prefer a public flogging to being absent from the prairie when dawn next cracks the eastern sky.

In tight little bands the antelope graze the prairie plants and nibble at the stems of newborn winter wheat. The bucks, it seems to me, like to put their colleagues between themselves and the road, and I suspect that many who didn't died.

It's evening when I turn off the highway and guide my rig up out of the gentle valley of the Musselshell River. Often, some well-chosen friend rides with me, but this year I am alone, and that's okay. Mule deer does already stand in the scrub pines, waiting for darkness to mask their assault on the alfalfa fields. Somewhere nearby the bucks are hiding, too smart to be seen along the road. And I know that here and there an empty-bellied coyote has already launched his night's hunt.

By the time I pitch the tent and set the Coleman two-burner to creating coffee, it is dark, and the howls of prowling

Pronghorn bucks on Montana prairie

Robert Winslow

Pronghorn buck in prairie grass

coyotes ring in the blackness. I'm tempted to take my predator call, walk two hundred yards from camp, and throw a phantom screaming rabbit into the night equation just to see what would happen. But something—is it fear?—holds me back. The night still belongs to the coyotes, and I'm content to let it be that way.

Later, I lie awake in my sleeping bag listening to the night sounds. The coyotes are quiet now, but an owl calls not far away. He's hunting a long way from the pines, I think. The grass rustles with animal movement, and I stop breathing to listen. But it is only mice a few inches away outside the tent. Later, something larger lumbers by, and I judge it to be a skunk. I fall asleep thinking of the antelope that must surely be just over the next hill.

Some people take one look at the treeless prairie and label it godforsaken country, but I could not disagree more. Many of my best outdoor memories will live forever in the dry washes and coulees and sagebrush of the prairie. Memories of wildlife and camaraderie and independence and ingenuity and beauty. I remember, once, stepping from the tent into predawn blackness and strolling a short distance across prairie sod. My breath turned to visible vapor in the chill air, and the grass, stiff with cold, crunched beneath my feet. After a few yards, I turned and looked back, but the canvas womb had already disappeared in the darkness. I was as alone as a person can be, alone with my thoughts. I must have stood there a long time, because suddenly (at least it seemed sudden) a growing glow lit the eastern sky. Now I could see the outline of a distant horizon and the great void that stretched from me to there. A moment later, the emerging sunlight danced off the frosty cloak of a million sagebrush plants. The feeling was eerily primal, like being present at the creation, and it could happen only on the prairie. I live in the mountains and have been to the coast, the desert, farming country, large cities, and even another nation or two. Each has its merits, but for honest-to-goodness elemental wonderment, I'll take the prairie.

Each fall, I take the handmade rifle my father gave me and forsake the mountains for antelope country. This is, I think, a pilgrimage. A catharsis. All my little problems come undone out here where every set of tire tracks is called a road and every ranch house an oasis. On the prairie, you always know where you are and how you stand in relation to everything else. Forests are ominous and mazelike and devious. Elk are sneaky. The prairie is straightforward and honest. The antelope see you and you see them. May the best creature win. Out here, where the nearest other human may be a day's walk away, a person is his (or her) own measure. The prairie builds character.

At dawn, I set out from camp on foot, discovering each new vista by way of the tiny saddles that connect what pass hereabouts for hills. The antelope are here, but they're spooky. The season has been open for two weeks, and these pronghorns have made the connection between people and guns. Again and again, their rumps flare white with alarm, and they speed off to safer parts.

Of the several ways to hunt antelope, the one that brings me closest to the essence of the prairie is slow walking—plodding tediously, keeping eyes a mile ahead, and peering often through the binoculars. Stay low crossing the little ridges. Glass every new vista. Sooner or later—sometimes miles later—I'll spot antelope.

And along the way I'll visit the prairie. Up from the grass rise a dozen sage hens, fighting to gain altitude. They look like nothing so much as a squadron of B-52s. Later, a jackrabbit bursts from beneath my step to go zigzagging away, leaving little puffs of dust lingering near the ground. Farther on, I pass a lonely spot where a rancher's cow has died. The scavengers have feasted here, and what they did not eat has returned to the earth. A few patches of dried skin and the skeleton are all that remain. Next year, the grass will sprout greener in this spot, and by the year after that only the bleached bones will tell of the death here. Dust to dust.

About midmorning, two antelope top a rise seven hundred yards away and begin to move in my direction. When they drop out of sight behind a tiny hump of ground, I take off running at an angle that should bring the three of us together. But I go barely a hundred yards before I lose my cover and am forced to hit the dirt. From here on, it's belly work.

You can't get any closer to the prairie than this. Again and again, from a prone position, I bring one foot even with the other knee, dig in that heel, and push. With each stroke, I slide ahead about two feet. The smell of sagebrush is strong, and it seems I can even taste it. Dust sticks to my lips. Droplets of sweat fall from my face and turn to little balls of mud in the dirt. My neck aches from keeping my head so low. Repeatedly, some part of my anatomy makes the acquaintance of cactus.

Finally, I have cut the distance to four hundred yards and decide to let the strolling antelope do the rest of the work. When they're three hundred yards out, I steady the rifle on a clump of sagebrush and wait with pounding heart. I calculate that the way they're walking, the pronghorns will pass within two hundred yards of me.

But I am wrong. From the north I hear the drone of a truck engine approaching. The antelope hear it, too, and they begin a slow trot to the west. Perhaps too many bullets have come from too many trucks. In a few seconds, they're completely out of range and moving fast. The rest of the day goes no better.

That night the stars come out across the big sky. From my camp on a little hill I can look in all directions and see only darkness. No glowing cities or flickering ranch lights to break the blackness. Alone in the tent, I wonder what it must have been like to live on this treeless land when your nearest neighbor—not to mention the doctor, store, and other essentials—were a day's horseback ride away. I wonder about the thousands who crossed the plains and the many who didn't make it and now lie covered with a century of prairie sod. I drift to sleep listening to the coyotes talk to the moon.

Coyotes. They are another reason I love the prairie. One morning on a previous hunt, as the sun struggled to clear the rimrocks, I chanced to spot one of the wild dogs before it saw me. I slid into a crack between two rocks, laid my rifle across my knees, and pulled off a glove. Gently, I sucked the back of my hand until out came the tenderest squeak of a spectral mouse.

The coyote immediately began an intense search for breakfast, winding back and forth through the rocks to my right. I squeaked again, and the predator homed in on me like a heat-seeking missile. Twenty yards away, however, it climbed a boulder to study the strange form lurking among the rocks where only a mouse was supposed to be. Its fur glistened in the new light and its eyes sparkled. For a long time, we studied one another, we two hunters alone there on the prairie. Eventually, the coyote decided that its ears must have been wrong—or perhaps that this mouse looked too big to tangle with. I glanced away momentarily, and when I looked back, the coyote had melted into the labyrinthine rocks and was gone.

The second day goes much like the first, and my efforts to get within range fail. By late afternoon, my enthusiasm has tired feet. I begin to walk less and spend more time on my backside peering through binoculars at the distant flats. Now and then I forget about antelope and marvel at the nearby rimrocks and the tenacity of the few scraggly pines growing directly out of them. I think about the evening photographer's light that in a couple of hours will paint the prairie hillsides gold. I begin to prepare myself mentally for the empty-handed trip home.

Then off to my right three antelope cross at a brisk walk into a broad ravine. As soon as they disappear, I begin a dogtrot toward the north, paralleling their course but keeping a low ridge between us. When I have gone half a mile, I come to a dry wash that wiggles off toward their route, and I take it. A couple hundred yards later the wash peters out, and I have used up all my tricks. If the antelope stuck to their original route, they should be coming my way. If they maintained their walking pace, it should be soon. If I'm lucky, they won't spot me first and run. The prairie is full of ifs.

Heart and Soul of the Prairie

IF EVER A CREATURE seemed designed by the Master Architect specifically and explicitly for the habitat it occupies, it is the pronghorn. Elk get along in the woods. Bighorns subsist on mountain meadows. White-tails adapt to farmland. But pronghorns are the prairie. Pronghorns have sagebrush in their blood, distance in their eyes, and the hot western wind in their nostrils. More than the coyote or prairie dog or rattlesnake, pronghorns are the quintessential prairie animals.

For uncountable eons, the atoms of these sleek and speedy creatures have rearranged themselves in an endless cycle—prairie to pronghorn to prairie to pronghorn. With each passing generation, this animal became more inextricably linked to the bunchgrass and sagebrush and alkali soil of its environment until, still millions of years ago, the two entities merged. Gradually, pronghorns became the prairie, and something of the prairie settled forever in pronghorn genes. People have uprooted pronghorns and plunked them down in other places—Florida and Hawaii, for example—but it just doesn't work. You might as well try to grow corn at the North Pole or get Herefords to give birth to hamsters.

Pronghorn fawn in spring grass, Montana

Likewise, prairie without pronghorns is little more than vacuous space, no matter how many lesser creatures make their livings there. Just as the night sky would be but a void without the moon and stars, America's vast plains would echo empty without the hoofbeats of teeming pronghorn herds. Pronghorns are the lifeblood, the central species, the heart and soul of one of the great wildlife habitats on earth. They are to the western American flatlands what caribou are to the tundra or wildebeests to the Serengeti. Pronghorns and prairie are one.

There are lots of reasons to like pronghorns. They are, for starters, incredibly beautiful animals. Because they occupy great stretches of open space, antelope can afford to eschew camouflage and go for the visual glory of exquisite, striking beauty. Their rusty browns and tans are overlaid with generous splashes of dazzling white. A forceful black provides the accents, and no two pronghorns are colored exactly alike. Picture this: A mature buck stands in the morning sun, light dancing off the white of his rump and the snowy signature bands of his chest and neck. The inky black of his nose and cheek patch speak of strength and dominance. Great horns arc high above his head, their polished tips nearly touching and the prongs jutting far forward. With his attention riveted on something far away, the buck's every muscle is on full alert, cocked and ready to fire. He stands tall and proud, ready to explode with speed or do battle with a rival. Can there be any doubt that this is one of the most magnificent animals on earth?

Pronghorns are to be admired, too, for their tenacity, their ability to thrive where lesser species would surely fail. They came once, a few short decades ago, to the edge of extinction, peered into that abyss, and abruptly stepped back. Today, they number about a million strong, flourishing on huge swaths of land that mere humans long ago wrote off as uninhabitable. They eat the weeds livestock will not touch and, if necessary, get by even without drinking water. No cold is too cold for the pronghorn, no desert too dry. They are can-do creatures, the adaptable children of twenty million years of perfecting evolution.

A multitude of additional antelope attributes strike the human fancy: the territorial rituals of the rut, the ability of fawns to vanish in the prairie grass, the bold attacks on would-be killers, the astounding vision, the unique horns, the social hierarchy of the herd, the inability to jump even low-slung fences, and on and on. Pronghorns are truly unique—and uniquely American. Born on this continent in the dim light of our distant past, they have outlived uncounted kindred species to become the preeminent prairie icon, the last symbol of the untamed West.

The one thing, however, that most endears pronghorns to people, that most excites interest in these animals, that most fascinates two-legged onlookers is the wondrous speed with which antelope move. When it comes to running, pronghorns are everything people are not—fast, explosive, enduring, sure-footed, smooth, fluid, synchronous. Antelope are the epitome of successful terrestrial movement. They have taken the power of a stooping falcon, combined it with the grace of a soaring eagle, added the quick turns of a backyard robin, and brought the whole package down to earth. They are, in the words of the old song, poetry in motion. Over any distance greater than a sprint, pronghorns are unquestionably the fastest land animals on earth, the very best runners that flesh and blood can create. Anyone who likes a winner will find great joy in getting to know these animals that are, quite simply, born to run.

CHAPTER ONE

What Creature Is This?

SCIENTIFICALLY SPEAKING, "ANTELOPE" IS not a scientific term. The word comes from the Greek antholops, which means something like "brightness of the eye." Used first to describe a mythical denizen of the Euphrates region, this name later became attached to a rather large group of cloven- (split-) hoofed ruminants (cud chewers). The world's true antelope are part of the group of hoofed mammals known as bovines. Their kin include bison, buffalo, cattle, sheep, and goats, but this family tree is a big one with lots of other branches. Details about horns, hooves, teeth, and other accoutrements help separate antelope from their relatives, but perhaps the best way to describe the distinction is simply to say that antelope are the more graceful, slender, delicate members of this clan (although this can be something of stretch, too, since the wildebeest and some of its colleagues are considered antelope).

As a group, antelope are a little like beauty and pornography—difficult to describe, but you know it (or one) when you see it (or one). In the very distant past, antelope were an even more eclectic lot than they are today. That's no small statement, considering that even now some antelope stand nearly as large as horses while others have a rabbitlike

Pronghorn buck in morning sun, western Montana

stature. In this country, many people are at the very least vaguely familiar with some of Africa's best-known antelope—eland, kudu, gazelle, impala, and a few others. Less well known are such animals as blackbuck, springbok, dik-dik, kob, bongo, oryx, and a lot more. There are, quite simply, a heck of a lot of antelope species in the world, about eighty-five in all. Antelope evolved in Africa and Asia and for the most part remained there, although a few made it into Europe.

However—and now we get to the point of all this—there are no native antelope in North America (or in Australia). The progenitors of many existing American wildlife species arrived here by crossing the Bering land bridge from Asia at some time in the distant past. One of the immigrants evolved into an animal that looked a lot like the many antelope species elsewhere in the world, but the single antelope to make the journey became extinct here long ago. (However, the oryx, an aforementioned African antelope, has since been introduced to New Mexico and maintains a wild population there.)

When the first Caucasians ventured into the American West, they encountered lots of wildlife they had never before laid eyes upon, including this swift, small, almost goatlike, brown-and-white, prairie-dwelling animal. These creatures had to be named, of course, and the designation the explorers chose was "antelope." This name made perfect sense to them, since they were aware of similar animals elsewhere in the world. The critter looked like an antelope. It acted like an antelope. It was obviously not a deer or an elk or a sheep. It did resemble a goat, but in North America wild goats lived in the mountains. So, probably without a great deal of thought, they said it was an antelope and went on to more important things.

And they could hardly have been expected to do any better. After all, this animal quite apparently shared many—perhaps all, as far as they knew—of the characteristics that made an antelope an antelope. What these early folks did not know was that the animals they had "discovered" did not possess one important attribute of other antelopes—hollow, permanent, unbranched horns. That's it. When it comes down to the scientific nitty-gritty, horns

Pronghorn doe with yearling fawns, Montana

are what separate America's "antelope" from the rest of the teeming herd (more about this in chapter 3).

Scientists, of course, knew that this American animal did not belong in the same seating section as the world's antelope (or deer or cattle, for that matter). In 1818, George Ord, a prominent zoologist of the time, studied the specimens of this slightly odd creature that Lewis and Clark had brought back from their western travels and proclaimed its Latin name to be Antilocapra americana, literally American goat-antelope. Officially, this tidied things up, but most folks ignored the "goat" part of the name and simply called the critters antelope. Some biologists threw a fit about having so prominent a large mammal so incorrectly named (even unofficially), but by then it was too late. The antelope name stuck. For the record, this animal's formal taxonomic pedigree is this:

Order—Artiodactyla (hoofed animals with an even number of toes)

Suborder—*Ruminantia* (cud-chewers)

Family—Antilocapridae (distinguished by horns, includes only pronghorns)

Genus—*Antilocapra*

Species—*americana*

Subspecies—*five* (discussed in chapter 14)

There was, however, a compromise of sorts. Since the horns of true antelope do not branch, the nomenclature nitpickers suggested that these American animals might be better named for the protrusion that distinguishes the male's headgear. Although not nearly so prominent as the multiforked antlers of deer, elk, caribou, and the like, the males do indeed exhibit a small tributary about halfway up the main horn. Too diminutive to qualify as a branch, this protrusion came to be called a prong, and so a potential new name was born—pronghorn. The sticklers for accuracy used this term exclusively, and even today you're likely to hear wildlife biologists speak of "pronghorns," not "antelope." Most everyone else, however, continued (and continues) to call them antelope, and so the two names have taken separate, though more or less equal, paths to legitimacy.

Not infrequently, you will also run into the redundancy "pronghorn antelope" (as if there were some other kind of antelope on this continent). Fuss not. Call them antelope. Call them pronghorns. Call them pronghorn antelope. Just don't call them slow, because then you're truly talking about some other creature. Generally, this book uses the terms "pronghorn" and "antelope" interchangeably, mostly for the sake of variety.

Male antelope are called bucks, and females are does, the same designations used for deer. The young have been referred to both as "kids" and "fawns," with the latter much more prevalent these days. In this book, they're fawns.

One final note about names: You may occasionally hear someone call these animals goats or prairie goats.

Mostly, it's hunters and ranchers who talk this way, and they don't mean any harm by it. In fact (though these folks would never admit it), they often use the term as one of begrudging endearment, as in: "Those damn goats are all over my ranch" or "Those goats have been giving us the slip all day." Though they often complain about antelope, most ranchers would consider the prairie an emptier, lonelier place without them. And hunters—the good ones, anyway—like to be challenged by a quarry capable of outwitting them. Calling the winner a goat helps even the score.

CHAPTER TWO

Antelope of the Ages

PALEONTOLOGISTS SAY THAT SOME kind of pronghorn has graced North America for twenty million years or so, ever since those first distant ancestors strolled across the Bering land bridge from Asia. These many predecessors came in lots of sizes and shapes, most looking little like today's pronghorn, and none related to the true antelopes of Asia and elsewhere. One or another of them sported four horns, stood two feet high, or had horns that spiraled to a point. One paleontological theory holds that modern pronghorns descended from a species with six horns (the prong on today's animal being the last vestige

of those multiple horns). At one time or another, at least thirteen pronghorn-like genera and probably dozens of species and subspecies roamed America, ranging from Florida to the Pacific Northwest and from Saskatchewan deep into Mexico.

Then came the Pleistocene epoch, with its huge ice sheets moving south from the polar cap. Gradually, inexorably, great changes came over the land. Some animal species adapted to these altered conditions and survived; others did not. Also about this time, the first humans—hunters by trade—showed up on the continent, and it's

Pronghorn buck in Wyoming prairie grass at first light

(Photograph by Lee Kline)

possible these early peoples also played a role in the changes that were to come. Whatever the cause, the ranks of the antelope menagerie began to thin, as one by one these species took dead-end turns in their evolution and vanished from the scene. Eventually, this process of elimination took its final victim, leaving intact just one antelope-like animal from the many that had once prospered. This is the animal we know today as the pronghorn, and it has changed very little over the last many millennia.

Native Americans came to know the pronghorn well, hunting it for food and revering its speed. In their own languages, they called this animal "small caribou" (Cree), "small deer" (Yankton Sioux), "pale deer" (Ogallala Sioux), and nearly twenty other things. The antelope also occupied a prominent place in the legends of many Native American cultures.

An Apache folktale suggests that antelope should not be hunted because long ago a beautiful young woman of the tribe became an antelope herself, and her descendants still run with the wild herd. The Hopi tribe believed the antelope to be a spirit messenger to the cosmic forces of nature and, therefore, full of powerful medicine. A Blackfeet legend tells how the pronghorn came to live on the prairie: The

Blackfeet god called Old Man created the antelope on the slopes of the Rockies, but when he turned the animal loose, its great speed caused it to stumble and fall on the rocks and fallen timber of the mountains. So Old Man moved his creation to the prairie, where it has gotten along quite nicely ever since.

Eventually, Europeans also became acquainted with pronghorns. History has not recorded the name of the first Caucasian to lay eyes on a pronghorn, but this person might well have been a member of the party commanded by Francisco Vásquez de Coronado, the Spanish explorer who toured the American Southwest early in the sixteenth century. Coronado landed in Mexico, then marched north to what is now Kansas. Along the way, his party encountered plenty of antelope. The group's official recorder, a man named Castenada, wrote, "There are many sheep and mountain goats with very large bodies and horns. Some [of the men] declare that they have seen flocks of more than a hundred together, which ran so fast that they disappeared very quickly." Since America also is home to mountain goats and bighorn sheep, it could be that Castenada is referring to them, but the references to large herds and great speed suggest that he is speaking of pronghorns.

Coronado, who was much more interested in gold than wildlife, simply noted in his journal, "There is a great abundance of wild goats the color of bay horses." Elsewhere, the party recorded seeing "siervos, remendos de blanco," which translates as "stags patched with white."

The expedition led by Meriwether Lewis and William Clark spotted their first antelope on September 5, 1804, in the region where the Missouri River today forms the boundary between Nebraska and South Dakota. Ten days later, Captain Clark shot one of the animals, and Sergeant John Ordway made this creatively spelled, punctuated, and capitalized record in his journal:

> *Capt Clark joined us had killed a curious annimil resembling a Goat Willard brought it on board. it was 3 feet high resembles a Deer in some parts the legs like a Deer. feet like a goat. horns like a Goat only forked Turn back picked hair thick & of a white and dark redish coullour. Such an animal was never yet known in U.S. States. the Capt had the Skins of the hair & Goat Stuffed in order to Send back to the city of Washington. The bones and all.*

Before long, virtually everyone in this new land got to know these somewhat odd-looking animals that they took to calling antelope. Anyone venturing onto the western plains could scarcely avoid their bountiful herds, which rivaled in numbers even the seemingly infinite bison throng.

Although reduced somewhat from prehistoric days, the pronghorn's range in recent centuries was still immense and included at least part of every state west of the Mississippi River except Arkansas, Louisiana, Missouri, and Washington. From the shortgrass prairies to the sagebrush flats to the deserts of the Southwest, antelope occupied a giant elliptical range that stretched from east Texas to western Minnesota to California's central coast. In Canada, they covered the prairie steppes from the Red River region in southeastern Manitoba all the way to the slopes of the Rockies in Alberta and even ranged as far north as Edmonton, Alberta. In Mexico, pronghorns roamed south to within a couple of hundred miles of Mexico City. One estimate put this animal's total range at two million square miles.

And just how many pronghorns were there in those Edenic days of American wildlife abundance? Estimating the size of bygone wildlife populations is a thoroughly inexact science, but one that historians and naturalists seem to relish. Since there was nothing remotely resembling a modern wildlife census then, the retro-tally takers have had to

rely on anecdotal descriptions and their own ability to extrapolate from whatever portion of the population they personally witnessed.

For starters, some early travelers in the West commented that pronghorns seemed at least as abundant as bison, whose overall peak population is sometimes pegged at fifty million to seventy million. In journal after journal, nineteenth-century writers describe antelope as "numerous," "abundant," "teeming," "thriving in great throngs," "almost constantly in sight," and on and on. One train passenger in the 1870s described a herd that stretched for seventy miles and contained an estimated one million animals. Another observer, identified in the writings of naturalist Ernest Thompson Seton as Major J. B. Bond, traveled by train from Denver to Cheyenne, Wyoming, in the winter of 1868–69. He wrote:

> *All the antelope had left the open plains and were now sheltering among the foothills. For 10 or 12 miles in [a particular valley] and all the way west of the train, about 3/4 to 1/2 mile away, was one long band of antelope, 20 to 40 rods wide, practically continuous, and huddled together for warmth. Their numbers changed the color of the country.*

Seton later seized upon this description and calculated that Bond's eyes had fallen upon two million antelope. He further estimated that these animals had likely migrated to this location from no farther than two hundred miles away, which with a little additional arithmetic gave him the square mileage of the throng's normal summer range. This, he calculated, constituted one-fiftieth of the total area occupied by all pronghorns. Therefore, Seton concluded, the antelope population at that time must have been about one hundred million animals.

Perhaps suspecting that this figure might be a tad generous, Seton approached the problem anew from an entirely different direction. By actual census, he discovered, there were in Great Britain in the year 1894 some twenty-five million sheep residing on eighty-eight thousand square miles. This comes to three hundred woollies per square mile. Having traveled in Britain, Seton made the observation that sheep in that nation appeared nowhere near as abundant as antelope on the American prairie. To allow for the greater visibility of antelope (due to fewer trees and hedgerows to hide behind, brilliant white rumps,

Pronghorn buck standing before Montana's majestic mountains

PRONGHORN: PORTRAIT OF THE AMERICAN ANTELOPE

and other factors), he slashed the estimated pronghorn density by a whopping 90 percent. This left him with an estimate of thirty antelope per square mile, on good range. Guessing that there were one million square miles of prime habitat and one million of mediocre habitat (which would support only half as many antelope), he arrived at a total population estimate of forty-five million pronghorns on the American plains.

If the same person can come up with two so disparate estimates, is there any hope of knowing how many antelope there truly once were? Probably not. Any other calculation is just as likely to be fraught with unproven assumptions and offhand guesses. For what it's worth, however, various other students of pronghorn abundance have guesstimated the species' presettlement population to be between thirty million and sixty million animals.

Whatever the number was, it soon began to decline. The ceaseless westward stream of settlers, miners, trappers, and others that defined much of the nineteenth century dealt the antelope a severe blow. Pronghorn meat was good to eat, free, and available just about everywhere in the West except the mountains. If travelers camped for the night and needed a meal, they might shoot an antelope and eat heartily but leave virtually all the carcass for the scavengers. If times got tough (and even if they didn't) on the settlers that drew homesteaders to the West, antelope became the meat de jure. If a rancher needed some bait to lace with poison to kill wolves, he shot a pronghorn. Anyone with extra ammunition might choose to try his or her luck on a pronghorn, leaving the animal to rot.

In all fairness, such behavior reflected the prevailing ethics of the day. The conservation mentality that is so much a part of modern life had not yet been born. This land was huge and its resources seemed as endless as the starry night sky. What was one antelope more or less when there were a few million more just over the hill? Today, of course, we decry such behavior—perhaps the same way our descendants may one day chastise us for such wasteful extravagances as watering lawns or distributing daily news printed on paper.

As cities sprang up across the West, market hunters filled wagons with dead antelope so these urban people might have food for their tables. In the early days of the California gold boom, pronghorn steaks fetched a whopping twenty-five cents per pound, but by the 1860s you could buy three or four entire antelope in the Denver market for that same quarter. When rail transportation became available, market hunters shipped tons of meat back East and to the growing settlements on the Pacific coast. In some places, pronghorns were so easy to acquire that professional hunters had a hard time giving their kill away. According to one report, a California market hunter set up shop near a popular pronghorn watering hole during a drought in 1859 and proceeded to slaughter five thousand of the animals as they came to drink. According to the report, this hunter took only the hides (which are rather inferior anyway) leaving the meat to rot.

The wanton obliteration of bison also hurt pronghorns. For eons, antelope had thrived side by side with endless herds of bison in an excellent example of peaceful coexistence. Bison preferred to eat the bountiful prairie grass, while antelope thrived on forbs, sagebrush, and other shrubs, but the relationship was a bit more complex than a simple mutual exclusivity of diet. Forbs—the broadleaf plants that are the staple of the pronghorn diet—grow best in open sunlight, a commodity that was sometimes in short supply beneath the undulating tallgrass prairie oceans. Bison, however, routinely cropped the grasses short, allowing forbs—and the antelope that ate them—to prosper. Typically, teeming masses of bison

Pronghorn buck feeding, Montana

17

passed through an area, overgrazing the grasses as they traveled. The forbs that prospered in the bison wake drew the attention of equally teeming herds of pronghorns that followed the bison herd by a year or more in an endless, ageless cycle. So, in a very real sense, antelope needed bison. Consequently, when human greed, stupidity, and ignorance reduced the seemingly infinite bison masses to a fragile few, the prairie grass once again grew long, and pronghorn populations suffered.

Antelope sustained additional losses from other indirect and unintended hits. Farmers who may have borne no particular ill will toward pronghorns nevertheless did antelope a great disservice by turning millions of acres of prairie sod upside down. They planted wheat and corn and other crops where prairie grasses once grew, and subdivided the wild prairie with fences that inhibited antelope movement. Roads and railroads chopped up additional historic range, and towns sprouted near many traditional pronghorn watering holes. Once, prairie fires regularly swept the plains, burning off the grass pronghorns didn't eat anyway and allowing the forbs they did eat to get a foothold. Settlers, of course, extinguished prairie fires at every opportunity.

The arrival of cattle and sheep on the western plains was a mixed blessing for pronghorns. Livestock, like the bison that preceded them, generally prefer grass over forbs, and so the ever growing domestic herds could have helped rejuvenate sagging pronghorn populations by filling the bison's role in keeping the prairie in prime condition for antelope. Also, ranchers often provided water for their livestock in places where none had previously existed, a change that made pronghorn life easier and tended to decentralize antelope populations.

Whatever assistance cattle and sheep might have rendered was largely eclipsed, however, by the fences that often accompanied these animals. Pronghorns typically do not jump fences (a topic covered in chapter 11), so each time a new wire barrier went up, antelope mobility and access to good range declined. Also, many ranchers mistakenly believed that antelope were taking food from their livestock's mouths—and money from their own pockets. Consequently, they considered pronghorns vermin to be eliminated whenever possible, a tenet frequently backed with action—and bullets. The ill-founded notion that antelope steal huge amounts of food destined for cow bellies became particularly destructive after America entered

World War I in 1917. For a time, killing antelope, thereby supposedly providing more beef for the troops, actually bordered on being a patriotic duty.

The truth of the matter is that antelope and livestock (especially cattle, but sheep as well) have relatively little overlap of diet. On some ranges, grass constitutes 85 percent of the bovine diet but only 10 percent of pronghorn fare. One study has even suggested that it would take 105 pronghorns to consume the same amount of cattle-appropriate forage as a single cow. (In terms of overall carrying capacity, however, the ratio would be much lower.) Also, pronghorns tend to be itinerant feeders, always looking for morsels that are just a little better than those presently in sight. This makes it difficult for antelope to overgraze the range, something that cannot be said for the plodding livestock.

For lots of reasons, then, antelope numbers declined steadily throughout the nineteenth century and into the twentieth. In 1908, a government survey put the total U.S. and Canadian antelope population at twenty thousand. Seven years later, the official estimate was fifteen thousand, but other observers put the figure closer to ten thousand animals. The documented decline of antelope in Colorado mirrored the national crisis: In 1860, that state had an estimated two million antelope. By 1898, those herds had been reduced to just twenty-five thousand animals. In 1908 they numbered two thousand, and by 1918 fewer than one thousand pronghorns remained in Colorado. South Dakota's estimated pronghorn population went from an estimated seven hundred thousand prior to 1800 to fewer than seven hundred in the early 1920s. Other states experienced similar declines, and across the country people began to write off the antelope as a lost cause. In just a few decades, pronghorns had gone from incredible abundance to virtual obscurity.

Late in the nineteenth century, however, groups of preservationists, sport hunters (as differentiated from market hunters), and wildlife aficionados began working to rescue the pronghorn. This was the start of what we now call the conservation movement. At its core was a flickering new paradigm, a novel way of looking at natural resources not as unlimited bounty to be exploited but as finite treasures to be preserved and protected and used wisely. Part of this emerging new ethic involved wildlife management, ecology, and the complex relationships between people and wild animals. Lots of species benefited, the pronghorn prominent among them. Local groups began working with landowners, encouraging them to tolerate more antelope. Researchers began casting a scientific eye at the relationship between pronghorns and people. And one by one, western states eliminated antelope hunting—North Dakota in 1899, Montana and Texas in 1903, Wyoming in 1909, South Dakota in 1911, and so on.

For a couple of tenuous decades, however, the antelope decline continued. Like a great ship whose momentum carries it toward the reef long after its engines have stopped, pronghorns moved ever closer to the edge of extinction. But the rescue effort was working, and sometime prior to 1920 the pronghorn's seemingly unstoppable march toward oblivion stopped just short of the extinction abyss.

Once the juggernaut of pronghorn decline ground to a halt, recovery was not far behind. Because pronghorn does usually give birth to twins each year, the species is capable of great fecundity. Relentless persecution had all but eliminated the prime pronghorn predator, the wolf. By 1924, the continental antelope population stood at thirty thousand animals, about double what it had been less than a decade earlier (although precious few antelope remained on some of the West's prime range—seven hundred each in Arizona, Utah, and South Dakota; two hundred in North

Dakota; twenty in Oklahoma; and ten in Kansas). A prolonged drought across much of the West during parts of the 1920s and 1930s discouraged the conversion of additional prairie sod to cropland and even caused some previously cultivated land to be abandoned and allowed to revert to shrubs and other antelope-friendly cover. The hunting moratoria in most states continued into the 1940s, and in 1937 the Pittman-Robertson Act (which taxed guns and ammunition, with the money earmarked for wildlife restoration) began making thousands of dollars available for pronghorn management.

Almost as fast as pronghorn populations had declined, they now increased as the fractured remnants of once-teeming pronghorn herds gave rise to new aggregations of antelope. Seemingly overnight, the prairies were again spotted with the distinctive white-on-brown signatures of pronghorn prosperity. Between 1924 and 1957, pronghorns in Wyoming increased from fewer than seven thousand to more than one hundred and five thousand. Montana's herd went from three thousand to fifty-nine thousand; New Mexico's from seventeen hundred to twenty-two thousand; South Dakota's from fewer than seven hundred to twenty-two thousand; Arizona's from six hundred and fifty to more than nine thousand. Colorado's herd rebounded to ten thousand. During the half century between 1925 and 1975, pronghorn numbers increased nationally more than 1500 percent to something approaching half a million animals. Today, the U.S. pronghorn population stands at about one million animals, a far cry from the bountiful millions of yesteryear, but still among the most plentiful large animals on the continent.

The recovery in Canada largely mirrored that of the United States, with the population going from about thirteen hundred in 1924 to twenty-two thousand in 1976. Today, the Canadian population is nearly fifty thousand.

Pronghorns have not fared as well in Mexico, although good tallies are sometimes hard to come by in that country. According to wildlife biologist and pronghorn researcher Jim Yoakum, the twenty-four hundred pronghorns thought to exist in Mexico in 1924 had dwindled to six hundred by 1983. In recent years, Mexican wildlife authorities have improved their pronghorn management program, relocated U.S. antelope to various Mexican sites, and beefed up protection of the two extremely rare pronghorn subspecies living in that country. The current best estimate is that pronghorns in Mexico number between fourteen hundred and fifteen hundred.

Overall, however, the pronghorn has enjoyed a long and incredible bountiful existence on this continent. While many other species have come and gone, this uniquely American has endured its way to true icon status. Few other wild species in the world have come to be instantly recognized around the globe as symbols of their lands: the elephant in Africa, the tiger in India, and the caribou in the Arctic, for example. Likewise, the pronghorn represents American wildlife to the world, and it is entirely fitting that it should be thus.

CHAPTER THREE

What Manner of Beast Is This?

FOLKS HAVE BEEN TRYING to pigeonhole the pronghorn since those first Caucasian eyes beheld the animal a few centuries ago. Their natural inclination was to compare this brand new species to something familiar, but because the antelope is so much an entity unto itself, comparisons quickly got bogged down. Naturalist Ernest Thompson Seton summed up the bewilderment early observers must have faced:

> *Like the giraffe, the American antelope has two hoofs [prominent toes] on each foot; like the goat, it has a gall bladder and a system of smell glands; like the deer, it has four teats and a coat of hair with an undercoat of wool; like the goat, it has hollow horns on a bony core; yet as in the deer, these horns are branched and are shed every year.*

Truly, the American antelope is a unique creature. It is part of the order Artiodactyla, which simply says that its hoof is divided into an even number of toes. (The pronghorn has two toes on each foot, but lacks the small pair of dew claws that adorn the lower legs of deer.) This order also includes cattle, camels, deer, sheep, and most other hoofed animals of that ilk. Pronghorns also are part of the ruminant family, animals that chew a cud and have

Pronghorn buck with three does in Arizona desert

(Photograph by Robert Campbell)

a complex stomach divided into compartments. Finally, antelope are further compartmentalized into the genus Antilocapridae. In fact, pronghorns define the genus, since they are the only species it contains. So, quite literally, the pronghorn is unique. Perhaps the best way to understand this beast is to consider separately some of its attributes.

SIZE

Many a pronghorn hunter, or anyone else with the opportunity to examine one of these animals up close, is surprised to discover just how small they are. Maybe it's because we so often look at them through binoculars. Or maybe because the vegetation where they hang out is usually rather short. Or because their legs are relatively long. Whatever the reason, antelope often appear to the casual onlooker to be more or less deer sized. Not so. In fact, the pronghorn's body is roughly the same size as a sheep's, although the antelope's longer neck and legs make it seem much larger.

Actual pronghorn dimensions vary somewhat, depending on the geographic region and the animals' diet. Biologist Jim Yoakum, considered one of the nation's top antelope experts, lists the following measurements for

average pronghorns. Larger (and smaller) individuals are not at all uncommon:

	BUCKS	DOES
Weight	120 pounds	105 pounds
Length	55 inches	55 inches
Shoulder Height	35 inches	35 inches
Ear Length	5.7 inches	5.7 inches
Tail Length	5 inches	5 inches
Horn Length	13–15 inches	3–5 inches

Somewhat surprisingly—or perhaps not so surprisingly, depending on how perceptive you are—an antelope's legs are about the same length as those of a cow, which may weigh seven or eight times as much. Nature does nothing without a reason, and it's probably safe to assume that long legs add to the antelope's speed and improve its vision by raising its head a wee bit above surrounding vegetation.

HORNS

Of all the things that make pronghorns unique, none is more important than the buck's pronged horns. In fact, it

Pronghorn buck displaying horns, western Montana

is this headgear that makes the antelope the sole resident of its own evolutionary cul-de-sac.

The antelope's distinction begins with the difference between horns and antlers. Ignoring the pronghorn for a moment, we can safely say that antlers are solid and horns are hollow. Deer antlers, for example, remain rock-hard all the way through, while cow horns ring as hollow as an empty promise. Also, antlers generally are shed annually and grown back again the following season, exclusively by males in most species. Horns are permanent and often worn by both genders, although perhaps in rather different forms. Horns also are unbranched (picture cows and bighorn sheep), while antlers may diverge into elaborate tributaries (visualize elk and caribou). Finally, antlers are made of bone (albeit solid and without marrow). Horns consist of keratin, the same protein of which hooves, claws, and fingernails are made. These rather straightforward rules of biology govern virtually all horned and antlered animals and have helped greatly in categorizing them.

Except for pronghorns. Pronghorns break these rules as easily as they violate speed limits. Buck antelope shed their headgear annually (part of it at least), so that gives them antlers—right? These things also branch, albeit minimally, into a main stem and forward-pointing prong—another vote for antlerdom. But wait. An antelope's adornments are made of keratin, and they're hollow (sort of). So they must be horns—yes? More than one nineteenth-century biologist lost sleep trying to make sense of all this, so don't feel bad if you're confused. What the experts have decided is this: Because of the stuff of which they are made, the adornments atop an antelope's head are indeed horns. But it is futile to try to squeeze the antelope into any category. This is, in fact, the only creature in the world to shed a branched horn annually. That's why pronghorns are the sole member of their genus.

Now, let's try to make more sense of all this, starting with who in the pronghorn world has horns and who does not. Buck antelope always do, with young males displaying their first protrusions (just little bumps, really) when they're about four months old. As seasons pass and the buck matures, the size of his horns continues to increase. Generally speaking, the bigger the horns, the older the buck, although the quality of an animal's diet can disrupt this equation. Does, on the other hand, may or may not have horns. About 40 percent do, although theirs generally rise no farther than three or four inches from the head and do not develop a prong.

Antelope horns consist of two distinctly different components, an inner core that few people ever see and an outer sheath, which is what most casual observers consider the horn. The latter, it has often been said, fits over the former like a scabbard over a saber. The core is pure bone and emanates from the skull just above the eye. The keratinous sheath is composed of hairlike material fused into a solid substance that feels almost as hard as bone, but definitely is not. Soon after the autumn rut, the sheath loosens and slips off. Beneath it remains the bony, prongless core, with the beginning of a new sheath already forming at its tip. Over the winter, the sheath grows in both directions from the core tip, until it joins the skull at one end and terminates in a graceful arc and sharp point at the other. By early summer, the new horn is complete.

Normally, a buck's horns angle slightly forward from his head, develop a forward-pointing prong about halfway up, and terminate with a pointed tip that arcs either toward the other horn or backward (or both). Sometimes they even arc forward. Likewise, there is a lot of variability to the horns' spread (the distance between them at the tips) and to the size, shape, and vertical location of the prong. Hunters measure antelope horns along the longest direct route from the base to the tip (ignoring the prong). Horns measuring around fifteen inches are considered pretty decent trophies.

Generally, things like horns and antlers have evolved into their current form for a good reason. Horns aid antelope in defense against predators, provide weapons for mating-rights competition, help impress and attract females, and perhaps serve other functions as well. But what of the prong? Why would antelope develop such a small branch for their horns? The answers to these questions are often speculative, with one possibility that the prong is designed to defend against the thrusts of other bucks. When bucks squabble over territory or does, the disagreement can escalate into head-to-head combat, and the well-placed jab of a horn tip can kill an opponent. Although it is in the long-term interest of the species to have the strongest, fittest bucks do most of the breeding, it does not necessarily follow that the losers should routinely suffer serious wounds or death. So, the theory goes, the prong helps a buck parry the dangerous thrust of an opponent. The more powerful buck can still assert his dominance with the force of his blows, shoves, and general strength, but the prong on the lesser buck's horn catches the thrust and prevents the tip

from inflicting a severe puncture wound. The prong, in essence, performs the same function as a sword's quillon; it protects its owner during duels.

Occasionally, nature bungles things, and a buck with odd horns shows up on the prairie. The two horns may angle toward each other and even cross. Or cross in front of the animal's face. Or there may be four horns instead of two. Another abnormality is droopers, horns that angle groundward rather than skyward. One Wyoming buck's drooped so severely that the poor creature could feed only by walking backwards. Apparently, this handicap made the buck especially skittish, and he managed for quite some time to elude the many hunters who were eager to bag such an unusual trophy.

HIDE AND HAIR

Antelope have extremely coarse hair, thick strands that are rather brittle and only loosely attached to the skin. Many a first-time antelope hunter, after dragging his trophy even just a short distance across the prairie, has been astounded to find nothing but bare skin where the animal had been in contact with the ground. And the leather itself is thin, porous, and of generally poor quality—not at all like the strong, attractive, and versatile deer hide. Certainly, the folks who settled the West found uses for antelope skins, but only because they had few alternatives.

Still, it took a long time for people to accept that antelope hides are of little use to anyone but antelope. When accurate rifles finally made it possible for market hunters to dispatch large numbers of antelope, some members of that profession set out to make a killing in antelope hides. The beautiful and contrasting colors, they reasoned, had a lot of customer appeal, and even if only the leather is considered, the virtually unlimited supply should bring in big bucks (the spending kind). So, with the intention of adding to the nation's supply of clothing, hats, tack, and anything else made of leather, the sharpshooters started mowing down antelope for their hides (although certainly in some cases the meat was used as well). Frontier entrepreneurs shipped tens of thousands of hides down the Missouri to St. Louis and points east, but the enterprise was a flop. As recently as the 1940s, however, people were still trying to make things from pronghorn skins (motivated by the war-engendered shortage of good leathers), but to little avail. Antelope hides look great as part of a trophy wall mount, but beyond that they hold little value for humans.

The antelope themselves, on the other hand, use their pelage to great advantage. Antelope hair, in fact, is one of the major reasons why these creatures are able to survive both the bitter cold of the northern plains and the extreme heat of the southwestern deserts. When winter rolls in with its subzero temperatures, the hair lies flat, layer upon layer, like rows of shingles. The biting wind of an Arctic front skips off antelope backs the way water rolls off a roof (or something like that). In hotter climes and times, the individual hairs stand almost totally erect, allowing air to circulate near the skin to draw off heat.

In addition, the individual hairs are themselves little wonders of insulation. Each hair is hollow, not solid, and contains a kind of spongy pith that is in turn filled with air. Although the amount of air inside a single strand is infinitesimal, cumulatively it adds up to a considerable blanket of insulation covering the animal's body. In his book *The Pronghorn Antelope and Its Management,* Arthur Einarsen tells of an Oregon State College zoologist who (some decades ago) tried to purge the resident air from some antelope hairs (for the purpose of photographing them). First, the scientist cut the hair into half-inch segments and soaked it in xylol for forty-eight hours. This did little to displace the air, so he put the hair in a low-water vacuum for an hour, with equally dismal results. Over the next three days, he also failed with a variety of high-powered vacuums. Next the researcher tried for an entire week to coax the air from the hair with warming. Still, most of the samples bobbed like corks when put into water, a sign that the air remained. The zoologist eventually got enough air from enough hairs to complete his experiment, but he came away with a renewed respect for the insulating qualities of pronghorn pelage.

Generally, antelope hair is an inch-and-a-half to two inches long, with the white rump hairs an inch longer and those of the mane up to another additional inch. The belly hair is shorter and softer, and that on the legs and face shorter still. Finally, at the end, there is a short tail.

Pronghorns molt in the spring, exchanging their dull winter coats for summer finery. As hair falls off in irregular patches during the molt, antelope acquire a worn, moth-eaten look, but by late summer new hair has replaced old, and pronghorn coats are again thick and shiny.

Pronghorns also make great communicative use of their hair. As every antelope hunter knows, these animals are adept at using their white rump patches as a kind of Morse code device, flashing signals to one another over distances of a mile or more. In addition, some researchers have suggested that the distinctive colors—and, more specifically, the color patterns—of pronghorn pelage could serve to confuse a predator, especially when it is in pursuit of a running herd of antelope. (These and other nifty little tricks are discussed in more detail in chapter 9.)

With photos speaking volumes, it is pointless to use feeble words to say much about the colors that make antelope unique, except to affirm that these are truly attractive, beautiful animals. Generally, antelope in northern climes are of darker hues than those in more southern regions, but the difference is slight. Although the striking brown-and-white contrast is hardly surprising in an animal so visually oriented, these patterns do have at least one unexpected attribute. Researcher David Kitchen, working with pronghorns on the National Bison Range in Montana, discovered that the splashy white markings on antelope heads, necks, and bodies are not all alike. In fact, each antelope's white pattern is usually distinctive enough to permit its identification, not unlike the personal facial features that make people individually recognizable. In his work, Kitchen carried with him a portfolio of photos of his study animals as well as a written description of each animal's markings. Using

Robert Winslow

this information (plus differences in the bucks' horns), he was able to successfully identify 100 out of 108 study animals. (More generally, a mature buck can be identified as such at some distance, both by its longer horns and its black muzzle and the black patch on its cheek where the lower jaw meets the neck.)

EYES, EARS, AND NOSE

Antelope eyes, measuring about two inches in diameter, rank as some of the largest in the animal world, bigger even than those of the horse and the ox (which outweigh the pronghorn many times over) and nearly as large as the elephant's. Pronghorn peepers also are more fully protected than most, set deep in their sockets and guarded by a protruding brow. Long eyelashes provide additional protection. These features may be adaptations to the brushy vegetation into which antelope often stick their heads. Less well-protected eyes might easily fall victim to a stiff branch or stem. Pronghorn eyes, colored an intense black, are set high on the side of the animal's head to provide panoramic vision. (The remarkable

Pronghorn buck in springtime molt

eyesight of these animals is covered more completely in chapter 9.)

The hair-covered ears are about five inches long, three inches wide, and terminate in a rather sharp point. Hunters sometimes use ear size to help decide if a distant antelope buck is of trophy quality, or whether it's a buck at all. Since a doe's horns are only three inches or so long, an antelope with horns shorter than its ears is almost always a doe or a fawn. If the horns are appreciably longer than the ears, the relative position of the prongs comes into play. The prongs branch from the main horns about halfway up, so if those projections are well above the ear tips, the total horn length may be approaching trophy status. Pronghorn hearing is rather well developed.

The antelope's sense of smell is also quite good, although as a warning device it plays second fiddle to this animal's truly amazing eyesight. In much of the wild world, the sense of choice is smell. But not with antelope. A pronghorn that smells an intruder may well postpone a bounding retreat until it can confirm the danger with its eyes. Conversely, a deer (and many other odor-oriented species) that locates potential danger with its eyes may choose to maneuver downwind to confirm the identification with its nose.

HOOVES

Antelope feet are not radically different from those of other two-toed hoofed animals, except that the front pair is larger than the rear. This anomaly perhaps developed so that the animal's weight might be handled better during its trademark high-speed runs. Another adaptation along that line is the cartilaginous padding that helps cushion the hooves against footfalls made on rocks. In addition to facilitating the pronghorn's renowned locomotion, antelope hooves make formidable weapons, especially when attached to an irate doe whose fawn is under attack by a predator. Antelope also use their feet to dig in the snow to find food.

A word of explanation is in order concerning the number of toes on most split-hoofed animals. The first digit—the one that would be comparable to the human big toe—is missing, lost somewhere on evolution's dusty backroad. The two middle toes have become greatly enlarged, forming what we call a cloven or split hoof (as contrasted with a horse's one-piece hoof). In many species, the remaining two outside digits have been reduced to small vestigial appendages set above the hoof on the lower leg. These are commonly called dew claws and exist on deer, cattle, and lots of other animals. But antelope have no dew claws, possibly another adaptation to all the running this animal does, since dew claws would be just one more thing to catch on the brush.

Blackfeet Indian legend has a different explanation, one that also demonstrates why antelope have gall bladders and deer do not. The story goes like this: Once upon a time, when both animals had both accoutrements, they met on the prairie and decided to bet their gallbladders on the outcome of a race. Naturally, the pronghorn won, and so the deer has been forever missing a gallbladder. But the deer demanded a rematch, complaining that the pronghorn had enjoyed an unfair advantage because the race had been run on the pronghorn's home turf. The second contest took place in the woods, and the antelope—perhaps a bit cocky at this point—agreed to wager its dew claws. Racing over fallen timber and brush, the deer won, and the antelope lost its dew claws.

TEETH

Antelope have thirty-two teeth, twelve on the upper jaw and twenty on the lower. There are no upper incisors. Rather than severing plant stems scissorslike between upper and lower incisors (the way a human might do), an antelope gets the same result by using its lower teeth to pinch the plant against its hardened, toothless upper gum. Chewing on plants that are often covered with dust, then chewing it all again as a cud, is hard on pronghorn teeth and can make tooth wear an unreliable indicator of longevity. Through age four, however, antelope acquire their teeth in definite stages, which allows anyone who knows the pattern to make a good estimate of an individual animal's age.

GLANDS

Ask any hunter or anyone else who has had close personal dealings with pronghorns—these are smelly creatures. They possess both a distinctive general fragrance that even dull-nosed humans can recognize at ten paces and a number of other odors that have meaning only to other antelope. Most of the latter emanate from one or another of the prong-horn's many glands. Prominent among these are the rump glands, which typically discharge an odor as an alarm signal at the same time the rump flares white. Some people claim the ability to smell this scent a hundred feet or more away. Antelope also have a gland between the toes on each foot (called interdigital glands) that produces a substance thought to help condition the hoof as well as deposit a scent with each footstep. In addition, a buck possesses two

Pronghorn buck marking territory by rubbing glands on shrub

33

subauricular glands (one on each cheek) and a median gland on the rearward center of his back. The cheek glands are closely tied to sexual goings-on, as the buck uses them to mark territory and advertise himself to does. He distributes the odoriferous identification from these glands by rubbing his cheeks on vegetation or any other available surfaces. The median gland is also thought to serve a mating function, possibly by adding a sexual scent to the warning smell of the nearby rump glands. Finally, pronghorns have slightly glandular regions on their hocks, the purpose of which is not entirely clear.

STOMACH

As a ruminant, the pronghorn possesses a complex, four-chambered stomach. Most mammals would have a tough time digesting a diet of almost pure cellulose with just the normal allotment of gastric juices in a run-of-the-mill single-chambered stomach. Humans, among other species, solved the problem by expanding their diets to include lots of things besides cellulose. Many of the grazing and browsing species, however, left the diet alone but changed the stomach.

Ruminants tend to eat fast and spend little time with initial chewing. The food goes first into the rumen (or paunch), where it is moistened. Then it passes into the second chamber, where resident bacteria and protozoans go to work reducing the stuff to a more digestible form. Later, the antelope regurgitates the food (now called a cud) from this fermentation vat and chews it thoroughly. When swallowed a second time, the material passes through the last two chambers and is assimilated. Although cud-chewing has the reputation of being a rather leisurely pastime, it is actually a go-go kind of activity, with the animal making more than a hundred chews per minute.

In a roundabout way, the antelope's ruminant stomach functions as a defense against predators. If a feeding antelope needs to, it can wolf down (pardon the expression) forage as fast as the mouthfuls can be separated from the plants. Later, from some prominent lookout point, it can regurgitate the food and chew its cud in relative safety.

VOICE

Though they usually don't have a lot to say, pronghorns do make vocal sounds. Anyone who has spent much time within earshot of these animals may have heard them utter a kind of snort, which is most likely the quick exhalation of air from the lungs. The Klamath Indians of the Northwest, in the common Native American manner of giving things descriptive names, called antelope cha-oo, which is said to have come from the almost sneezelike sound they sometimes make. Fawns use a short, high-pitched, quavering bleat to summon their mothers or to complain about one thing or another. Does communicate to their offspring with a sort of grunting bleat, and bucks sometimes use a dull roar to express their aggressive mood. Courting bucks also make several whining, lip-smacking sounds during courtship.

SLEEP

Antelope can be active day or night, although they appear to get most of their business done during daylight hours, with peaks of activity just after dawn and at dusk. They sleep (lying down) intermittently around the clock, probably never for more than a few minutes at a stretch. In the distant past, pronghorns prone to sound snoozing became the meals that made wolf bellies fat, and in this way nature eventually created a species of nappers, not deep slumberers. Every few minutes, each antelope awakens to take a quick glance around for danger. Seeing none, it may doze again, but never so deeply that it would miss the alarmist stirrings of some other members of the herd. Some observers also

have speculated that upon awakening an antelope will notice any changes that occurred in the scenery during its nap (such as that a rock that looks like a hunter is now twenty yards closer). This is difficult to document, however.

MORTALITY

The normal pronghorn life span is somewhere in the neighborhood of nine years, although a few individuals may live past the age of fifteen. The record is eighteen. These figures can be misleading, however, since lots of antelope die as fawns, and the life expectancy of a buck in a hunted population probably is no greater than four or five years. Human hunters, predators, disease, harsh winters, droughts, and accidents are the main causes of pronghorn mortality.

Studying antelope in Oregon over a three-year period, biologist Jim Yoakum discovered that half of all pronghorn deaths occur among fawns not yet six months old. Specifically, he found that 38 percent of the 225 dead antelope he located had perished during their first two months of life. Another 12 percent died between three and six months of age, 8 percent between seven and eleven months, and the remaining 42 percent between one and ten years. It seems, therefore, that if a fawn can survive to

the tender age of six months, it has a decent chance of becoming an old-timer.

The causes of pronghorn deaths are fairly obvious and straightforward. Predators—especially coyotes, but also bobcats, and on occasion several others—kill plenty of antelope. Usually, their victims are fawns, and in some studies predators have claimed up to 50 percent of a year's fawn crop. Since pronghorns and rattlesnakes share so much habitat, these reptiles almost certainly kill a few pronghorns, although antelope have been known to return the favor by stomping rattlesnakes to death. Disease takes some antelope lives, but pronghorn herds are well known for their lack of epizootics (although unconfirmed reports suggest that a massive and undiagnosed die-off may have occurred across antelope country in 1873). Likewise, antelope are usually rather free of parasites. Winter occasionally exacts a heavy toll.

Accidents are another threat. One March, authorities found about one hundred dead antelope at the base of a remote forty-five-foot cliff in the northeast part of Wyoming. They speculated that the animals had stumbled off the precipice during a blinding storm. Now and then, a train or a wheeled vehicle will plow into a herd of antelope that, for whatever reason, can't get out of the way. In one Oregon accident, an automobile driver wiped out eighteen of the animals, plus eighteen more in the wombs of the pregnant does that were among the victims. In Wyoming, a truck once dispatched forty pronghorns and a train about one hundred; in each case, the animals had congregated on the road or track during the winter, probably because it was the only place around where the snow was not prohibitively deep.

PRONGHORN SPIRIT

Like all other living things, antelope are more than the sum of their parts. With the breath of life steaming from their nostrils, they become a special beast, superbly adapted for life in their chosen habitat. No dissection will ever find or isolate or label that greatest of all antelope attributes, the pronghorn spirit.

Pronghorn buck on sunset stroll, National Bison Range, Montana

CHAPTER FOUR

Born to Run

IMAGINE, IF YOU WILL, an animal Olympics. The event is running, and every continent, habitat, and wildlife family has conducted extensive preliminaries so that the creatures assembled at the starting line represent the fleetest four-legged animals on the face of the earth. (Two-legged competitors were eliminated long ago.) The starter's gun goes off, and the contestants burst from the line in a tight pack. At first, several animals—including the rabbit, the gazelle, and the greyhound—appear to be in the race, but after relatively few bounds they are left behind. The cheetah moves to an easy lead, gliding with

long, seemingly effortless strides ahead of the deer, horse, pronghorn, and other hoofed animals. Then, just a few hundred yards from the starting gate, the cheetah begins to flag, to run out of gas. Some of the hoofed speedsters pass the cat, but before long all but one of them begins to fade as well. Barely half a mile into the race, the pronghorn surges to the lead on powerful, rhythmic, sustainable strides no rival can match. And this athlete is just getting warmed up. If competition rules required it, the pronghorn could run like this for miles, leaving all other contestants gasping for air in the distant dust. In all but the very

Pronghorn buck running across Montana prairie

shortest of races, the pronghorn clearly owns the title "Fastest Runner on Earth."

The antelope is indeed an animal athlete—a world-class, gold-medal, go-for-broke speedster. Native Americans, who for centuries had to hunt antelope on foot or at best on horseback with bows and arrows, were painfully aware of this. And it did not take long for Caucasian explorers of the West to realize that this strange creature was truly in a class by itself. In September 1804 in what is today South Dakota, Captain Meriwether Lewis recorded this encounter of the fastest kind (in his own creative kind of spelling and syntax):

I had this day the opportunity of witnessing the agility and the superior fleetness of this animal [pronghorn] which was to me really astonishing. I had pursued and twice surprised a small herd of seven [and finally] got within about two hundred paces of them when they smelt me and fled; I gained the top of the eminence on which they [had] stood, as soon as possible from whence I had an extensive view of the country. The antilopes which had disappeared in a steep reveene now appeared at the distance of about three miles on the side of a ridge. so soon had these antelopes gained [this] distance [that] I doubted at ferst that they were the same [ones] as I had just surprised, but my doubts soon vanished when I beheld the rapidity of their flight along the ridge before me. it appeared rather the rappid flight of birds than the motion of quadrupeds. I think I can safely venture the assertion that the speed of this animal is equal if not superior to that of the finest blooded courser. ["Courser" can refer to either a swift dog or horse. There is no way to be sure which one Lewis had in mind.]

Humans have always admired speed, and even casual antelope watchers want to know just how fast these animals can run. Early in this century, writer and naturalist Ernest Thompson Seton, forever fond of devising clever ways to quantify things, set out to calculate the pronghorn's top speed. He attempted this by counting the number of bounds an antelope makes in a minute, measuring those leaps, and doing the necessary arithmetic to arrive at a miles-per-hour figure. His conclusion was that antelope (at least the ones he tested) travel at thirty-two mph, two mph slower than the horse. Many other veteran pronghorn watchers, supported by lots of anecdotal accounts, think Seton's antelope were running with the brakes on.

Ever since humans began building machines capable of pronghorn-class speed, the drivers, engineers, and pilots of these conveyances have been pitting their contraptions against antelope. Many a dust cloud on many a country road marks the spot where antelope, for whatever reason, have chosen to race a car—and what driver would not accept the challenge. Consequently, pronghorn literature abounds with eyewitness accounts of these animals keeping pace with a moving car, train, or airplane at amazing miles per hour: thirty mph for seven miles. Forty mph for three miles. Fifty-five mph for half a mile. And the granddaddy—seventy mph (over an unspecified distance). Someone even claimed to have clocked a crippled pronghorn doing thirty-five mph on three legs.

Many of these observations, however, should probably be taken with a stiff skepticism chaser. Many occurred decades ago, when some cars would have had trouble keeping up with antelope. Any driver going fifty or sixty or seventy mph over the prairie, even on the kind of road that typically exists in pronghorn habitat, would likely have his or her hands full just staying alive, let alone watching a nearby antelope. And, of course, there is the human penchant for exaggeration.

One incident, however, appears well documented, comes from reliable sources, and doesn't totally stretch the limits of believability. Consequently, it gets cited more often than any other and is generally accepted by unscientific antelope enthusiasts as the last word in the measurement of pronghorn speed. Here is Arthur Einarsen's account from his book *The Pronghorn Antelope and Its Management*:

On August 14, 1936, I was with a group that paced many pronghorns on the dried bed of Spanish Lake in Lake County, Oregon. This lake bed was as hard as adobe. It was a clear, breezy day...ideal to stir the racing instincts of the pronghorns, and as we rolled along the lake edge we had many challenges. Small groups here and there raced beside the car, until five, led by a magnificent buck, ran parallel to us, pressing toward the shore from the feeding area in the lake center while we drove on a straight course. As they closed in from the right, the buck took a lead of about fifty feet and Meyers [A.V. Meyers, field observer for the Research Unit at Oregon State College] increased speed to keep even with the animal. Dean Schoenfeld [W.A. Schoenfeld, dean of the School of Agriculture at Oregon State] watched the speedometer, Myers drove the car, and I photographed the moving animals. The buck was now about 20 feet away and kept abreast of the car at 50 miles per hour. He gradually increased his gait, and with a tremendous burst of speed flattened out so that he appeared as lean and low as a greyhound. Then he turned toward us at about a 45 degree angle and disappeared in front of the car, to reappear on our left. He had gained enough to cross our course as the speedometer registered 61 mph. After the buck passed us, he quickly slackened his pace and when he reached a rounded knoll about 600 feet away, he stood snorting in graceful silhouette against the sky as though enjoying the satisfaction of beating us in a fair race.

Many modern scientists of speed have trouble accepting Einarsen's account. Generally, these researchers have concluded that under good conditions pronghorns can probably travel at thirty or forty mph for several miles and that some individuals may hit appreciably higher speeds over short distances. Sixty mph, however, remains rather suspect. To break sixty, say the number crunchers, an antelope would have to take consistent strides of twenty-nine feet each, a feat that one group of scientists called "beyond the pronghorn's ability." Approaching the question from another angle, Stan Lindstedt and his colleagues (more about them in a moment) used the pronghorn's oxygen consumption rate to estimate its sustainable speed at forty-five mph. So the debate continues.

But does it really make any difference? Whether Einarsen's account is totally accurate or not is anyone's

guess, but the image of a great pronghorn buck proudly passing a car at breakneck speed is a delightful one indeed, even if the observers might have fudged a little on the details. Does it really matter whether this buck—or any other pronghorn—actually hit sixty-one mph? Or fifty-nine? Or fifty? That antelope are the fastest runners on the continent—and the fastest in the world over any appreciable distance—is not in question. There simply are too many unassailable accounts of high-speed pronghorns to challenge that claim.

The animal with which the pronghorn is most often compared for speed is the cheetah, that great predatory cat of Africa. The cheetah, it is often said, is the fastest land animal on earth (several birds travel much faster), sometimes topping seventy mph over short distances—probably very short distances. In a race any longer than a sprint, the pronghorn would win hooves down. And among more closely related creatures the antelope truly has no peer—or even near peer. Top speed for a horse is about thirty-four mph, and a white-tailed deer likely maxes out at about twenty-five mph.

In many ways, even more amazing than the pronghorn's flash point speed is its endurance, its astounding ability to run faster than any other animal on earth mile after grueling mile. Sure, they need quick-start speed to distance themselves from attackers, but why have they developed a marathoner's ability to run at nearly top speed from one horizon to the next?

Part of the answer may lie in the tactics employed by one of the pronghorn's most feared traditional predators, the wolf. Cougars, bobcats, and the rest of the cat clan generally catch their prey in short, powerful bursts of speed that they cannot long sustain. If a prey animal can sprint well, it stands a good chance of escaping from a feline. Wolves (and other canines, too) are different. Wolves are the marathoners of the predatory world, sometimes pursuing prey doggedly (how else?) over great distances. These carnivores even have been known to chase their victims in shifts, with a fresh wolf taking over just as its colleague begins to tire. (A detailed account of a coyote doing the same thing is offered in chapter 8.) If antelope were to survive on the American plains, where wolves hunted by the thousands, they not only had to have great initial acceleration, but also had to be enduring runners. So that is how they evolved—quick out of the starting gate and still going strong miles later. At least that's the theory.

Gray wolf, a pronghorn predator, Montana

Pronghorn buck running, Montana

Recently, comparative physiologist Stan Lindstedt and several colleagues set out to analyze the antelope's amazing ability to run. Do these animals, they wondered, possess some kind of secret weapon, some undiscovered bombshell of anatomy that makes them the fastest things on four legs over any significant distance? To find out, the researchers outfitted two captive pronghorns (a pair of orphaned fawns provided by the Wyoming Department of Game and Fish) with breathing masks and got them running at twenty-two mph on a treadmill—which, by the way, had to be set at an incline because on level ground the machine could not stay ahead of the antelope. By measuring the animals' consumption of oxygen, the buildup of lactic acid in their blood, and other characteristics, the researchers were able to quantify at least some components of pronghorn quickness.

The results, simultaneously fascinating and a little disappointing, clearly indicate the absence of any kind of secret antelope weapon. There are no hidden steroids in sagebrush, it seems. Instead of being vastly superior in any one aspect of running, pronghorns are simply a little better at almost everything affecting speed. In organ after organ and system after system, antelope display small advantages over similar animals. No one of these adaptations, by itself, makes a crucial difference, but combined in a living, breathing antelope they collectively spell the difference between just another run-of-the-mill runner and amazing speed.

For starters, the pronghorn is a dynamo of oxygen consumption, a kind of bestial gas guzzler that consumes great quantities of the invisible fuel that powers nearly all living creatures. In fact, their rate of oxygen consumption is fully three times greater than that of other similarly sized animals. To get all this fuel into the engine, pronghorns have evolved a relatively massive windpipe that can measure nearly two inches in diameter (compared to three-quarters of an inch in a human of the same weight). Likewise, pronghorns sport huge lungs (three times larger than those of comparably sized goats) and an oversized heart. In addition, pronghorn muscle cells are packed with mitochondria, the structures that actually burn the oxygen.

Incidentally, the pronghorn's voracious appetite for oxygen leads to a common misconception about its stamina. Hunters and other observers have for centuries noted that antelope almost always run with their mouths open and their tongues hanging out. Other animals do this, too, but usually just when they are tired. Many a pronghorn watcher has therefore assumed an antelope was about ready to drop, when in reality the animal was still going strong. An antelope, it turns out, hangs its tongue from its mouth not because it is exhausted, but to allow more air to pass through. Had those observers looked closely, they probably would have seen the mouth agape and the tongue lolling to the side with the animal's first steps.

But the antelope's adaptations for running go well beyond oxygen efficiency. The hooves are padded to minimize shock. The liver is large to provide a quick dose of glycogen. The digestive system is compact to eliminate extra weight. The legs are solid and compactly muscled, with the lower portions consisting mostly of bones and ligaments that are not easily injured. (By the way, the pronghorn's rear legs provide most of the go power, while the front ones, with their larger hooves, are used primarily for balance and steering.) Virtually everything about pronghorns has been adapted over the eons for speed and endurance.

Okay, pronghorns run fast and far, but how do they manage to pound for miles across hard, rocky, uneven prairie without breaking a leg or a neck or even just stumbling? Imagine for a moment that you are somehow suddenly blessed with the ability to race pell-mell across this same terrain on your own two legs at speeds from thirty-five to sixty mph. You'd likely fear for your life. So how does an antelope do it so routinely?

Knowing its home range the way you know your back-yard certainly helps. And perhaps a pronghorn's extraordinary vision allows it to spot the precisely perfect place to put down each galloping hoof (although this is pure speculation). A more studied part of the explanation lies in the remarkable strength of this animal's slender legs. Some years ago, C.E. Thomas, professor of engineering materials at Oregon State College, set out to test the relative strength of the leg bones of the cow and the pronghorn. He rigged an apparatus that would accommodate increasing pressure, strapped a foreleg bone from each animal in place, and began piling on the pounds. At 41,300 pounds per square inch, the bovine bone gave out. The antelope leg, however, held out for another four thousand pounds. (And keep in mind that the cow's bone was much larger.)

In the 1940s, Einarsen used casual observation to identify a number of pronghorn gaits, including those he called the "sedate walk," "leisurely trot," and "sudden bounding leap." More recently, researchers at the University of Lethbridge in Alberta also set out to quantify locomotive prowess. First, they went afield and filmed a number of antelope running at various speeds and gaits. Then, in the lab, they reviewed the film in slow motion and stop-action, magnified frames to show additional detail, and noted every possible variable about the animals' movements. They documented no fewer than thirteen pronghorn gaits, ranging from the "very slow diagonal walk" to the "lateral gallop" (the fastest). In the latter, the rocking motion characteristic of some other gaits disappears, as the antelope does everything possible to maximize its speed. The head drops down, the ears lie back, and the torso remains low and smoothly parallel to the ground. The length of each stride increases to about eighteen feet and sometimes as much as twenty-three feet.

Although it has little to do with speed, antelope sometimes employ a gait (if it can be called that, since there is little lateral movement) that takes most witnesses by surprise. It's called stotting and consists of the animal springing into the air and landing on all four feet simultaneously without really going anywhere. The closest familiar maneuver might be the mule deer's springy pogo-stick run, but at least the mulies seem to be headed somewhere when they do it.

Some African antelope species also are stotters, and the movement has been documented as well in elk and bighorn sheep. Biologists believe that stotting may function as a warning to enemies, perhaps conveying the message "I see you, and I can run pretty fast, so there's no point chasing me." If the predator takes heed, it saves the antelope the energy expense of a full-fledged escape. Almost certainly, however, stotting carries additional meanings, since it is sometimes used when there are no predators around.

Pronghorns often exhibit another odd bit of behavior (odd by human standards, anyway) when testing their legs against cars and other man-made machines. If, stretched out at a full gallop, the antelope is able (or allowed) to pull ahead of the vehicle, it frequently chooses to cross directly in front of its competitor. Left to right or right to left—it doesn't make any difference. An antelope that takes the lead simply has a profound—and sometimes death-defying—need to be on the other side. Maybe this is its way of saying, "Hey, buddy, the race is over, and I won." As you might guess, this can be a dangerous maneuver when a herd of any size is involved. Not all antelope are created equal, and while the leaders may cross well in front of the vehicle, stragglers could find

themselves eyeball to headlight with a car or suddenly aboard a Chicago-bound train. Automobile drivers, of course, can give the animals a brake, but locomotives can't. Such accidents are rare, however.

Pronghorns sometimes display a similar kind of ineptitude—and a much more dangerous one—when fleeing from a hunter. Imagine that a hunter shoots at and misses a member of a herd that is, say, 150 yards distant. The animals break and run, but instead of going as fast as possible directly away from the hunter, they run in an arc around the person, perhaps even through 180 degrees of the circle. Though shooting at a running antelope usually is a fool's endeavor (especially at that distance), some hunters feel compelled to blast away, and occasionally an antelope may be hit, although often not the one the shooter was aiming at.

Startled pronghorns don't always react this way, but they do often enough that the behavior is not really an anomaly. One theory is that they become confused by the shot's echo and don't really know from whence the sound has come. This explanation seems a bit strained, however, since there are few echoes on the prairie (because there are few vertical surfaces for sound to bounce off of). Another notion is that the animals hear the bullet hit beyond them

(assuming the shooter missed) and are running away from that sound. Still another suggestion holds that for eons antelope fears have focused on wolves, coyotes, and other carnivores that were of little danger as long as they could be seen and kept at a distance. It just may be that antelope running in an arc around a hunter are simply keeping the enemy in sight and not allowing it to come any closer. (They have to learn about bullets.) Perhaps over the next few million years this behavior will disappear, as fewer of those who practice it, compared to those who run straight away, live to produce young. (Presumably, the circuitous escape route selected in these instances eventually takes the antelope to some safe territory.)

Finally, the question arises of whether antelope run for fun. To be sure, they enter most races in a quest for survival, not glory or pleasure. Many biologists would probably say that adult pronghorns run only when they have to, only when danger, sexual stirrings, or some other necessity spurs them on. (Fawns, however, often engage in running play, an activity described in chapter 10.)

You don't have to be around these animals very long, however, before you get the feeling that they truly like speed, and history is full of accounts of antelope apparently choosing to race a steed, car, train, or whatever just for the sport of it. Intuitively, it is indeed difficult to imagine an animal with such ability that would not occasionally run just for the sake of running, that would not occasionally streak off across the plains just for the joy of it. Is it too much to think that when the prairie air hangs cool and crisp that pronghorns do not rise from their beds, stretch, and race off across the dewy morning grass at top speed, the sunlight dancing off their ebony horns, just because it feels good? Why would a sleek pronghorn in its prime not want the wind to whistle by its ears as it flies along at fifty or sixty mph? Or want to hear the rhythmic pounding of its hooves on the prairie sod? Or to burst with bestial pride at being the best there is? Biologists may scoff at all this, but as surely as sunrise, this happens. It has to.

Pronghorn herd on the run across Montana prairie

CHAPTER FIVE

Three Is Not a Crowd

SOMEWHERE ALONG THE LINE, every successful wild species chooses (evolves) a lifestyle that works, that allows its individuals to survive in their environment. Those that didn't all carry the same label—extinct. And what works for one species may prove disastrous for another. Survival involves many elements—what to eat, where to find food, reproduction rituals, rearing of offspring, predator avoidance, and on and on. One of these building blocks stands out, however, as perhaps the most defining characteristic of any species' lifestyle. We call it sociability. It's the difference between a throbbing, pulsating beehive and a lone butterfly flitting among flowers. Or a solitary eagle and a giant flock of starlings. Or a lone white-tailed deer and a herd of antelope. Above all else, pronghorns are creatures of the crowd, groupies of the first order.

Animals that live in heavy cover (white-tails, for example) can protect themselves by hiding, and when seclusion is the order of the day, fewer is better. It's tough for several large animals to hide very well together for very long. Consequently, white-tails—and lots of other species—are relative loners.

On the prairie, however, things are different. Seclusion

Pronghorn herd in Big Sky country

here, for an animal as big as a pronghorn, is impossible. So antelope long ago opted to become social animals, to live together communally, and to protect themselves not by hiding but by running fast. If you see one pronghorn, you're quite likely to see another, and even if you do not, there's a good chance that more are somewhere nearby.

The central unit of pronghorn society is the herd, but antelope organization is much more complex than this simple term suggests. Within that rubrical umbrella exist several subgroups composed of individuals meeting specific age, gender, and assertiveness requirements. To further scramble the situation, the formation and dissolution of these groups are highly seasonal phenomena. And even within a group there often exists a hierarchy that makes one seemingly equal animal dominant over another.

_____

Pronghorn bucks, doe, and fawn at watering hole in Wyoming

In the spring, the large winter aggregations of antelope break up, with each herd returning to its traditional warm-weather stomping grounds. Here, some mature bucks (generally those at least three or four years old) claim territories that they will defend against all male comers from now through the autumn breeding season. Bachelor bucks—those without the experience or assertiveness to claim territories—gather in itinerant bands and make a summer profession of testing the authority of territorial males. Does assemble in their own groups, often on the protected terrain of a territorial buck (or bucks). Later, the fawns of the year will become part of this assemblage. All this categorization, however, is not as rigid as it might first appear, with the membership of most groups remaining rather dynamic and sometimes changing almost hourly.

Social hierarchy is a key element in virtually all prong-horn groups—and it starts early in life. Before they are three months old, fawns begin sparring (generally without inflicting injuries) with their classmates to establish dominance rankings that may well stay with them their entire lives. By the time a doe reaches adulthood, she likely has settled into her own particular spot in the hierarchy, a position that probably will not change much over the years.

Of course, a new crop of yearling would-be social climbers must be worked into the pecking order each year, and it is not unheard of for a younger doe to displace a more senior counterpart in the hierarchy.

Nonterritorial bucks create the same kind of system, although theirs is often more fluid and unsettled. Bucks are forever challenging those above them in an attempt to work their way up the social ladder and claim one of the ultimate prizes—territory or a harem (or both).

To demonstrate its dominance, a superior antelope may spar with a subordinate or push it away from a choice feeding, watering, or bedding area. Usually, the subservient antelope will concede its relative weakness by assuming a submissive posture (ears, horns, and other elements in a decidedly neutral position) that is universally recognized in the pronghorn world. Or, it may simply move away as commanded. Or it may allow the dominant animal to mount it (without any sexual goings-on).

Most interactions between relatively equal does are initiated by the dominant individual, and most have no motive other than to the reaffirm the pecking order. In other words, the dominant doe does not really want the bed, bush, or other treasure being commandeered. She is just putting the underling in her proper place. Male interactions, however, are often initiated by a have-not, subordinate buck that would desperately like to improve his status. Buck confrontations serve the added purpose of determining which males will eventually do the breeding.

With a herd's hierarchy established, antelope life remains relatively peaceful throughout most of the year. Without this pronghorn pax, all manner of squabbles might occur to distract these animals from their eternal vigilance and the daily toil of making a living. Like humans, antelope have made compromises to facilitate social living.

Except for the rut. In autumn, reproductive urges override a lot of antelope sociability during a kind of every-animal-for-himself/herself melee. Lesser, want-to-be-landowner bucks incessantly pester their territorial superiors, and bachelor bucks try to horn in on the breeding. Does become flighty and unpredictable. Most of this action, however, occurs during an intense period of a few weeks. After that, everyone once again tolerates everyone else, with bucks that just weeks earlier might have fought to the death now feeding calmly almost side by side.

In winter, large numbers of antelope often congregate in the same area (sometimes traveling significant distances) to take advantage of forage, light snow cover, or protection from the elements. These aggregations are not herds in the hierarchical sense, but rather consist of several herds occupying the same terrain. When the climatic times get tough, antelope largely ignore social structure and seemingly keep the peace with a mutual agreement to hold interactions to an absolute minimum. It is as if they realize that energy expended in social struggles is energy that cannot be devoted to survival. Within these assemblages, however, individuals from a given herd tend to interact mostly with their own herdmates, possibly because life is easier when everyone knows where everyone stands.

Some form of antelope social structure even remains intact when the group is running for its life. At the initial alarm, herd members may launch a rather helter-skelter flight away from the danger (or at least in a wide arc around it, a quirk discussed in chapter 4). Soon, however, a pattern emerges, as individuals fall into their predetermined spots. Typically, the does go first, possibly with the highest ranking one in the lead. (Perhaps she also is the wisest, savviest member of the group, but only the antelope themselves know this for sure.) Then comes a group of younger animals, including fawns and some yearlings. Finally, the buck (or bucks) generally bring up the rear. If the herd fails to get properly ordered during the initial flight from danger, it will likely do so during the let's-look-back-and-see-what-scared-us stops that fleeing pronghorns often make. Naturally, there are lots of exceptions to all this, but generally antelope like order in their retreats.

Even when a herd is running full bore in what appears to human eyes a pell-mell escape, those dozens of feet may actually be hitting the ground in synchrony. When researchers at the University of Lethbridge in Alberta, Canada watched slow motion films of running pronghorns, they discovered that often every animal in the group was leading with the same foot (left or right). The running herd's lead frequently changed (from left to right and back again), but when it did, the entire group would be back in synch after just a few strides.

Incidentally, even when a herd appears to be running at top speed, each antelope (except, perhaps, the slowpoke of the group) is likely pacing itself so that the herd travels as a unit in its trademarked elliptical shape. Scientific analysis aside, pronghorns on the move are the four-footed incarnation of a sweeping, flowing, wheeling, flock of birds that somehow manages to move as if it were one being. Biologist

Bart O'Gara tells of hiding one day near a tangle net (designed to hold antelope without injuring them) concealed in the Nevada sagebrush. Chased by an airplane, about eighty antelope came thundering at top speed toward the barrier. "When the lead animal got within five or six feet of the net," says O'Gara, "she saw it, and that whole herd turned like a school of fish, did an about-face, and raced back the way they had come." None of the animals fell, and it appeared to O'Gara that they didn't even so much as bump shoulders. "They don't make many mistakes," he says.

For pronghorns (and many other species), communal living represents a mixed bag of advantages and disadvantages. On the downside, many animals together can attract predators that might miss a single animal. Food must be shared. Diseases can be easily communicated. And to prevent endless intraspecific squabbles, a strict social order and certain other behaviors must be observed. For example, antelope must be careful to avoid prolonged eye contact with one another, since staring often is interpreted as a hostile act. Sometimes, herd members even choose bedding positions that prevent even casual glances while resting. Likewise, does avoid eye contact with bucks during the rut,

since simply looking at them can elicit unwanted courtship activities. (At some point, of course, does in estrus become receptive to males.)

On the plus side of communal living, the more eyes and ears there are, the sooner enemies will likely be detected. And when predators do give chase, the chances of any individual antelope surviving are good (provided it is healthy), since the attackers have a whole herd of potential victims from which to choose. Also, a running herd may confuse a predator in ways a single fleeing animal would not. When breeding season rolls around, there is no need to travel to find a mate. Males have access to many females, and does can choose from among several bucks. Togetherness may not be for everyone, but it works well for pronghorns.

Because pronghorns are polygamous, they must maintain larger populations (in any given area) than might otherwise be necessary. If all mature bucks participated in the breeding more or less equally, the gene pool would remain diverse, and the overall local population could afford to be rather small. But when only a few bucks do most of the breeding (as happens with antelope), the population must be fairly large in order to ensure genetic diversity. (Sport hunting helps establish this diversity by creating a rather rapid turnover in the buck population.)

In a sense, the pronghorn is a tradition-bound species. All other things being equal, pronghorns are likely to occupy good habitat indefinitely, and the animals on that range today are quite likely the descendants of those that grazed there in seasons past. Knowledge of a herd's home range becomes a kind of communal property that gets passed down from one generation to the next through social living.

Pronghorn herd in Montana winter

CHAPTER SIX

Rituals of Reproduction

Like so many other things about this animal, the process by which existing pronghorns make more pronghorns is complex and fascinating—from the selection of mates to the intrauterine battles of competing embryos (described in chapter 10).

Most does breed for the first time as yearlings, when they are about sixteen months old, although occasionally a female fawn will mate during her first autumn (at the tender age of five months or so). Males are physiologically capable of breeding as yearlings, although few of that age ever get a chance to do so, because of their inability to compete with older, more experienced bucks. Most bucks are at least three or four years old when they breed for the first time.

The two genders also have evolved very different strategies for passing their genes on to future generations, the overriding goal of all wild creatures. Bucks employ a broadcast strategy and attempt to sow as many seeds as possible. By breeding any and every doe that will accept him, a buck increases the odds that at least some of his descendants will survive to carry his genetic heritage far into the future. In his lifetime, a successful buck could father scores of offspring.

Does, on the other hoof, are more interested in quality

Pronghorn buck herding doe during rut, Montana

than quantity. At most, a doe will produce only about a dozen fawns in her lifetime. Consequently, her reproductive strategy is to mate with the strongest, most impressive buck she can find. So, while bucks are commonly given credit for collecting harems of does, it often is the doe that chooses the buck and not the other way around.

Throughout much of the antelope world, controlling territory is everything to a buck. If he is the owner of a good chunk of territory, a buck becomes a breeder, a link in the age-old chain connecting past pronghorn generations to future ones. Without territory, he may be just another antelope on the prairie—and probably a frustrated one at that. For many bucks, success is simple and straightforward: Physical dominance allows them to claim and defend territory. Owning territory attracts does. The breeding of does is the sole measure of success. Period.

Competition for breeding rights begins in the spring when the largest, most assertive bucks claim territories to defend as their own. A good parcel, often shaped by features such as ravines, streambeds, and hills, may cover as much as a square mile or two (which is a huge holding among animals that actively defend their borders). The best territories also include adequate food and water, the proper topography for visual scrutiny, and the presence of other antelope. Bucks often seem to employ a bit of precognition (or maybe just a great memory) by selecting territories that are most likely to harbor good forage in the fall, an important breeding season attraction for does. Often, small tracts of no-man's land separate territories, which helps reduce the number of border disputes between adjacent landlords.

Unable to defend all his borders simultaneously, a buck posts olfactory "keep out" signs at the edges of his domain. One of these territory-marking behaviors is so ritualized that biologists have created an acronym—SPUD—to describe it. SPUD stands for sniff, paw ground, urinate, defecate. Obviously, this maneuver leaves behind the odors of elimination, but pawing the ground also is thought to deposit secretions from glands in the buck's feet. More glands in the buck's cheeks produce additional smells, which vigorous rubbing deposits on sagebrush and other vegetation.

Does are allowed access to a buck's territory, but other bucks are evicted, even long before breeding season arrives. Subtle, smelly warnings may be enough to deter younger and smaller competitors, but when one buck thinks he has a shot at acquiring another's territory (or, later in the year, at raiding his harem), it takes action to evict him. At first, the landowner buck may greet the intruder with nothing more than a stare, the penetrating kind of gaze that teachers use to stop misbehaving students in their tracks. This glaring encounter may last as little as ten seconds or as long as twenty-five minutes, and sometimes it is enough to convince the interloper to go elsewhere.

More likely, however, the territory owner is forced to take the intruder to task with a loud utterance that is a cross between a snort and a wheeze, accompanied by heaving sides and erected hairs on rump and mane. More timid intruders (usually the younger ones) may effect a retreat at this point. If not, the territorial buck comes closer, ready to do battle. Nature, however, discovered long ago that it would do the species no good to have bucks physically fighting all the time, so the territorial buck is first likely to engage in posturing, threats, false charges, and other kinds of noncontact bluster. In this escalation of hostilities, he may display his horns and cheek patch, grind his teeth, thrash nearby brush with his horns, and SPUD.

If, after all this, the would-be territory (or harem) thief remains, he is likely to find himself on the receiving end of an angry charge that is definitely not a bluff. This escalation usually is sufficient to send the trespasser packing, sometimes

Pronghorn buck marking his territory

61

with the resident buck hot on his tail all the way to the territorial boundary. (Interestingly, if the chase crosses out of one buck's domain and if the chasee happens to own the adjacent territory, a spectacular turnabout may ensue. Suddenly, the retreating buck becomes the property owner, the pursuer becomes the interloper, and the whole procedure may be repeated with the roles dramatically reversed. The power of territory ownership is that great.)

On occasion—usually one involving rather equal bucks—an intruder may choose to stay and fight instead of flee. Horns are the weapon of choice here, as the combatants maneuver, thrust, and try to gore one another, not unlike humans in a fencing duel. Or, if the bucks lock horns, the dispute may look like a sumo wrestling match, with each combatant trying to push the other backward and off balance. To acquire an advantage in this, experienced bucks maneuver to gain the higher ground so they can push downhill at the enemy. Periodically, the pair may break contact only to go at it again with renewed fury.

Typically, such fights last only a few minutes, but injuries, usually from puncture wounds, are common. If a horn happens to penetrate an opponent's heart, lungs, or other vital organ, this may indeed have been a fight to the death. Although major battles are rather rare, skirmishes are not.

In one study, nearly a third of the adult bucks were either limping or missing patches of hair by the time the rut ended.

(It is fascinating, too, to note how nature attends to details. Species that fight the way pronghorn bucks do often have built-in defenses to help minimize injury. The branched antlers of elk and deer tend to interlock, thereby reducing the number of punctures. The prongs on a buck antelope's horns serve the same purpose. Mountain goat billies, which because of the way they do battle tend to jab one another most often on the rump, have extremely thick skin in that region. Likewise, the skin of pronghorn bucks is thicker in the head and neck areas where they are most likely to get jabbed.)

Most of the time, the territorial buck is successful in defending his domain, which seems to indicate a kind of home-court advantage. Perhaps it is just that pronghorns (like many people) often work harder to defend something they already have than to acquire something new. At any rate, territorial bucks are only infrequently evicted. Territories change owners primarily through attrition. If, during the winter, a dominant buck dies, gets sick, breaks a leg, or in some other way becomes incapable of holding territory, a new proprietor takes over, perhaps after beating out other rivals.

Or, a newcomer to territorial ownership may get his

hoof in the door by appropriating the vacant land between two existing territories or by claiming a distant (and therefore poorly defended) corner of an occupied territory. In areas that are heavily hunted, territorial turnover can be very high, since most hunters prefer to shoot the larger bucks that are likely to be territory deed holders.

By itself, owning land has no value to the territorial buck. After all, breeding, not Monopoly, is the name of this game. But the two are inextricably linked. When the rut is in full swing, any number of males without territories of their own (called bachelor bucks) might endlessly pester a free-roaming doe. In one study, the amount of time does spent lying down (resting) went from 40 percent in the summer to 24 percent during the rut. All this extra activity consumes a lot of energy that can make a doe weaker and less well prepared for the coming winter. Consequently, does seek out a territorial buck (or bucks) to provide them with some measure of defense against would-be suitors. Ergo, a buck that can successfully defend territory may almost without additional effort assemble a harem. Not coincidentally, it also is in the doe's best interest—indeed, the best interest of the entire species—to mate with the biggest, strongest, most fit buck she can find. By doing so, her genes stand a better chance of existing in perpetuity.

Although bucks may defend territories throughout the spring and summer, actual breeding does not occur until August or September in the primary antelope range. The rut's starting date varies with latitude—earlier in the South and later in the North—and is triggered by the declining hours of daylight.

As the rut begins, several changes occur. Does become flighty and may rotate their presence among the territories of several bucks. Naturally, each male tries to prevent them from leaving his territory, but the wiles of the female usually prevail. According to biologist John Byers, a travel-minded doe may distract a possessive buck by urinating. Then, while he is preoccupied with an olfactory analysis of this deposit, she dashes off. Eventually, however, the does settle down to spend their time with a single buck, probably the one with which they will later mate. An extremely successful buck might control a harem of up to fifteen does, although the group could number as few as two or three. (Generally, harems are larger in the South and smaller in the North.)

Also about now, the sometimes sizable summer bands of bachelor bucks break up into miniherds of just a few animals each, which then patrol the range looking for does to kidnap. Territory owners, which have largely allowed does to come and go as they pleased all summer, now get interested in herding them and creating—and keeping— a captive harem, a chore they often perform with energetic, classic cow-pony hazing maneuvers. As border intrusions by guerrilla would-be breeders increase, the workload of territorial males becomes incredibly heavy, sometimes almost entirely without rest. Researchers once watched a territorial buck for about thirty-six hours over nineteen days of the rut. During that time, the buck spent less than four minutes lying down and was involved in one activity or another 93 percent of the time.

Researchers have documented virtually every aspect of pronghorn courtship. A territorial buck keeps a close eye on his assembled harem, frequently checking each doe for the onset of estrus by smelling her genital region and sometimes by taste testing her urine. Using a behavior called flehmen, the buck turns his lips in an outward curl and with his tongue moves a small bit of the doe's urine into a special nasal organ for chemical appraisal of the doe's estral status. If the doe permits it, the buck will attempt to mount her. If she is not yet ready for mating, the doe discourages her suitor either by twisting her head sideways in a recognized ritual of rejection or simply by walking away.

Eventually, the right time arrives. The buck advises the doe of his intentions with a high-pitched whine that smoothly declines into a low roar. His body becomes taut, his legs stiff, and the hair of his mane erect. Approaching the doe with short and prancing steps, the buck waves his head from side to side, perhaps to impress her with the size of his horns and the quality of his black cheek patch. Head waving also may reduce the chance of direct eye contact, a sign of aggression in the antelope world. He emits a low, staccato, sucking sound, which researchers think may be intended to appease the doe by mimicking the noise made by a nursing fawn. The buck brushes the doe's rump with his brisket, then mounts her. After several difficult months of competition, vigilance, and maybe violent battle, the mating process culminates with a copulation that typically lasts just a few seconds. Immediately, the participants lose interest in one another, with the buck going off to check the receptiveness of other does in his harem. This is the last significant contact the buck will have with the doe he has just bred, as males play no part in the rearing of fawns.

This territorial mating model is the classic pronghorn system described by lots of researchers, many of whom did their work in parks or with captive herds. For a long time, prevailing thought held that pronghorn procreation had no other significant wrinkles. Now, however, biologists know that dominant bucks don't always stand their ground and defend territory. On plenty of occasions, the system of using territories to allocate breeding rights breaks down, but a substitute is waiting in the wings, as documented by biologist John Byers at the National Bison Range in Montana in the 1980s.

Buyers found that for several years the number of defended territories declined, as a herd that had formerly followed the antelope textbook gave up this supposedly traditional mate-gathering technique. Instead, most bucks now became intruders bent on stealing does from the relatively few bucks that still stuck to the territorial strategy. With available does packed into fewer harems, the competition increased intensely, and the intrusion rate grew seventy-one times higher than before. The remaining territorial males spent virtually all their time chasing off would-be doe thieves. As soon as a landowner buck evicted a competitor from one side of his domain, he would have to race to the far side to deal with another interloper. Then another and another. "Soon the [male was] caroming around his territory like a ball on a billiard table," says Byers. Once, he watched a buck spend an entire day fending off fifteen intruders spaced more or less evenly around the perimeter

of his territory. In the end, this beleaguered animal gave up and surrendered his harem.

Some bucks retained their holdings by radically shrinking the size of their territories, although they usually lost some does in the process. With most bucks no longer participating in the territorial system, many does and bucks began pairing one-on-one and wandering to remote parts of traditional pronghorn habitat on the NBR. Other bucks still collected does and fought to keep them, but as itinerant bands, not on defended ground. For all intents and purposes, these pronghorns had totally abandoned their former mating system.

Puzzled, Byers began searching for the cause of this dramatic turn of events, but traditional explanations, such as a change in population density or food availability, failed to solve the mystery. Finally, after diligent research, he found the "smoking gun" source of the problem. Several years earlier, fierce winter weather had rolled into Montana, killing an unusually large number of territorial bucks, animals that had been weakened by the rigors of the rut. (In autumn, territorial bucks are the clear winners, but victory sometimes exacts a high toll. The nearly constant vigilance required to keep a doe harem intact leaves little time for the

buck to feed and strengthen himself for the coming winter. If the cold season turns especially ruthless, it is the dominant bucks that may be the first to succumb.)

In just one year, the ratio of does to bucks went from essentially one to one to almost four to one. Furthermore, every buck over the age of five had perished (NBR personnel thoroughly documented the winter kill), leaving only inexperienced males that probably had never before held territories. The subsequent birth of many male

fawns quickly brought the sex ratio back into line, but the tradition of defending territories had vanished with the older bucks.

Other researchers also have documented a pronghorn mating system based on the bucks' defense not of territory, but of the does themselves. Some observers now believe this to be the more widespread method, especially in areas

Pronghorn bucks sparring during rut, Montana

where hunting is common. In protected populations (such as in parks where biologists do a lot of pronghorn research), territoriality may indeed prevail. Where antelope are heavily hunted, however, sportsmen—like winter weather—may cull many older bucks, thereby triggering the other system.

Actually, there are advantages and disadvantages to each of these methods. Without a perimeter to defend, non-territorial bucks need to worry only about the does they possess, which greatly reduces the terrain they must cover. Freed from guarding the home front, these bucks can now travel wherever necessary to find does, eat, drink, or avoid danger. Because does usually do not enter estrus until late summer or early fall, these landless bucks can wait until then to devote precious energy to harem building.

Territorial bucks, on the other hand, often begin defending their estates in spring and continue to run off intruders through the autumn rut, an extensive period of calorie-consuming activity. For better or worse, they are wedded to that specific chunk of terra firma. But this isn't always a handicap. The season of perimeter defense has taught most other bucks to avoid the domains of territorial males, so that by the time breeding season arrives, much of

the work may already be done. And because territory owners offer does safe haven from all other bucks, the females willingly seek them out, relieving the males of some of the labor of harem gathering.

Also, any buck with a harem but not a territory becomes an immediate magnet for every would-be-papa pronghorn in the neighborhood. Bachelor bucks, wanting very much to add their genes to the reproduction pool, may charge the harem in the hope of scattering the does and copulating with one of them before the harem master can respond. Or, they may follow like beggars after the harem, hoping to breed one doe while the harem buck is busy with another. Although such tactics are not often successful, they can cause the harem owner a great deal of stress.

Regardless of how it is conducted, the rut ends with amazing abruptness. A few days after the last copulation, bucks that have been vigorously defending territories or harems abandon their holdings and join groups of mixed ages and both genders. Interactions of all types diminish, and pecking-order behaviors decline. Soon, the bucks' horn sheaths fall off, and the herd may join with others to form a winter aggregation. Next spring, however, they'll start it all over again.

CHAPTER SEVEN

Oh, Give Me a Home

FEW OTHER ANIMALS ARE so unmistakably identified with a single habitat as are pronghorns. White-tails today live just about anywhere, and mule deer often show up in surprising places. So do bighorns. And branches of the bison and caribou clans, long known for their open-space preferences, have even taken up residence in the forest. But antelope seem forever destined to remain where they evolved—on the prairie. It is almost as if the Creator produced prairie and pronghorns with the same sweep of that great hand.

Although most pronghorn habitat exists on the country's vast western flatland or intermountain valley floors, antelope have been known to live at elevations up to eleven thousand feet in Wyoming and Oregon. Most herds, however, are found between four thousand and six thousand feet above sea level, invariably where the terrain permits them to see great distances.

Generally, pronghorns live in areas that receive from ten to fifteen inches of moisture annually, and too much water is as bad as too little. If a lot of this precipitation comes in the form of forage-covering snow, antelope may have a tough time making it through the winter.

Pronghorn doe in prairie grass

(Photograph by Robert Winslow)

Their pointed hooves are good tools for finding food beneath the drifts, but when snow cover goes much beyond a foot in depth, chances for survival diminish significantly.

Temperature extremes bother antelope very little. These animals are endowed with an insulating coat capable of protecting them in all but the most excruciating cold. Conversely, pronghorns also are eminently capable of withstanding the scorching heat of the desert Southwest.

With the exception of Washington, pronghorns currently occupy at least part of every western state, as well as portions of two Canadian provinces and three Mexican states. The estimated continental population has for a decade or more been about one million animals, although this figure fluctuates with weather, range conditions, time of year, and other factors. With about 384,000 pronghorns (1993), Wyoming has by far the most antelope. Montana is second with 126,000 (1993). Other recent state estimates are as follows:

Arizona	14,500
California	7,000
Colorado	58,000
Idaho	21,500
Kansas	13,000
Nebraska	4,700
Nevada	15,000
New Mexico	30,000
North Dakota	7,800
Oklahoma	550
Oregon	22,650
South Dakota	47,000
Texas	14,534
Utah	7,000
Alberta	22,314
Saskatchewan	27,274
Mexico	1,450

(A note about these figures: Wildlife censuses are far from exact. Animal numbers ebb and flow over time, so the best we can hope for are estimates that might offer a current population snapshot that becomes almost instantly outdated. Over the long term, however, estimated population figures can provide valuable information about trends in a species' well-being. Consequently, the numbers above are intended to show the relative abundance or scarcity among the states and provinces, not to suggest that any one of these jurisdictions has [or ever had] the exact number of pronghorns listed. The total of these estimates, about 824,000, is less than the one million figure that is commonly used to quantify the continental antelope population. This is largely due to recent declines in Montana and Wyoming, decreases that quite likely are already being erased by pronghorn fecundity. Many of the above estimates come from a survey done by biologist Bart O'Gara and represent a population snapshot taken in 1989. Several others are 1993 or 1994 figures, and one [Idaho] is from 1986.)

Antelope use a host of plants—everything from bluegrass to thistles. Any herd's particular mix of food depends on the latitude, climate, topography, elevation, soil, moisture availability, and other factors of the region in which it lives. Researchers have found that antelope dine on at least 124 plant species in central Montana alone, and over the vast expanse of pronghorn range more than four hundred plants find their way into antelope bellies.

In one Colorado study, researchers found the antelope diet to consist of about 42 percent forbs, 43 percent browse (woody, brushy plants), 4 percent grass, and 11 percent cacti (more on this in a moment). These ratios can vary widely, however. Other researchers, for example, have found shrubs (browse) to constitute 71 percent of the pronghorn diet.

Pronghorn doe in prairie grass

Common forb species consumed by antelope include clover, alfalfa, wild onion, lupine, dandelion, mustard, buttercup, and larkspur. The shrub portion is dominated by sagebrush but can also include saltbrush, bitterbrush, and rabbitbrush. Cheatgrass, wheatgrass, timothy, and bluegrass are among the grassy entrees that antelope consume, mostly in the spring or fall. So dependent are pronghorns on forbs and shrubs, however, that they would perish if forced to live exclusively on grasses, which don't provide enough protein and certain other nutrients for the rather small (and therefore demanding) pronghorn digestive system. In general, an adult pronghorn must consume about two pounds (dry weight) of forage each day.

Although most antelope today do not live in major sagebrush country, this plant has become synonymous with pronghorn and their habitat. Sagebrush, in many minds, is the prairie, and antelope have long been inseparably associated with it. The truth is that other vegetation, notably nutritious forbs, is more important to most antelope most of the time than sagebrush. Still, this smelly shrub plays a crucial role in many antelope lives. In sagebrush, antelope conceal their fawns, seek refuge from winter winds, dodge predators, fill their bellies, and in other ways make their living. Sagebrush, which is surprisingly high in protein, provides considerable nutrition for antelope, especially in winter when little else may be available. It also sticks up above all but the deepest snowbanks, making itself available to pronghorn palates year round. So vital is sagebrush that herds on good sagebrush range have been known to survive severe winters while other nearby antelope confined primarily to grasslands perished.

Antelope prefer vegetation at an average height of no more than fifteen inches, and when much of the cover reaches thirty inches, they often quit using an area. This is probably due to their insatiable need to see, rather than smell or hear, what is happening. White-tailed deer and elk (both very odor oriented) may be perfectly satisfied to hide out in thick brush, but not pronghorns. Tall vegetation makes a coyote's stalk easier and a hurried escape less fleet, and pronghorns want no part of it.

One study in Idaho even found that antelope fawns in taller, thicker cover fell victim to predators more often than fawns in shorter vegetation. The explanation, it seems, is that predators—most of which are shy, secretive animals—prefer to travel and hunt in thicker cover and are therefore more likely to find pronghorn fawns hidden there. Also, an antelope doe aggressively trying to defend her fawn may stand a better chance of success in open areas where she can maneuver. Other studies, however, have indicated that more fawns may indeed survive in taller vegetation, so other factors may be at work here.

Unlike many of their relatives, antelope are delicate feeders that use both smell and touch to select only the tenderest parts of each plant, then move on to the next. Cows and many other large animals typically grab a mouthful of vegetation and pull, often uprooting entire plants in the process. Pronghorns, on the other hand, bite cleanly and neatly, leaving most of the plant intact—no small feat for an animal that lacks (as all ruminants do) incisors on the upper jaw.

This, coupled with the pronghorn's peripatetic nature, virtually guarantees that antelope (in normal numbers) will not harm rangeland. They appear to be forever on the move in search of that perfect morsel. More than one observer claims to have seen a calmly feeding antelope suddenly interrupt its meal to trot a half mile or more across the prairie seemingly just to sample the fare at some other location.

Of all the plants that make it onto the antelope menu, none is as—well—weird as cactus. Yes, pronghorns eat cactus. Topping even the Colorado cactus consumption mentioned earlier, pronghorn researchers in a Kansas study found that cacti constituted 40 percent of the diet among their study animals. Sometimes, antelope paw off the prickly spines, but on other occasions they eat the whole plant. Biologists speculate that antelope eat cacti mostly for the water these plants contain. In addition, pronghorns occasionally eat other weed species that livestock generally find repulsive (and sometimes dangerous), including cockleburs, thistles, snakeweed, and goldenrod.

Most pronghorns require free water—water they drink directly from some kind of pond, stream, or tank. Under normal conditions, a herd might travel once or twice a day to the nearest watering hole, although they seldom remain long at these spots because of the likelihood that predators also will visit there. In one Wyoming study, each pronghorn consumed, on average, slightly less than a gallon of water per day in May and slightly more than a gallon per day in August. The researchers also found that 95 percent of the twelve thousand-plus antelope they saw from the air were within four miles of water—a mere sprint in the antelope world. Pronghorns long ago learned to make use of water provided by ranchers for their livestock, and they have been known to

kill themselves trying to get through a pronghorn-proof fence to reach water on the other side. (If given the opportunity, antelope also will lick salt from blocks set out for cattle.)

These adaptable animals also get a lot of their moisture from the plants they consume, which is one of the main reasons they're able to occupy such arid habitat. In fact, the endangered Sonoran pronghorn subspecies (and perhaps the peninsular subspecies as well) may get along without any free water at all. Other subspecies also have been known to forgo the drinking of free water, even when it was available, if the moisture content of their forage was high enough.

Although pronghorns are overwhelmingly dry land creatures, they (like most other animals) swim naturally and do not hesitate to cross major rivers and other water bodies if they have a commanding need to be on the other side. Lots of people have no doubt seen antelope take to the water, but the first such recorded observation probably belongs to Sergeant John Ordway, who traveled with Lewis and Clark and wrote the following in his journal on April 26, 1805:

Pronghorn buck in high desert country, Montana

Saw a flock of Goats [pronghorns] Swimming the [Missouri] river this morning near to our camp. Capt Lewises dog Scamon took after them [and] caught one in the River. Drowned & killed it and Swam to Shore with it.

One final note about pronghorn habitat: A lot of antelope range is owned by the federal government (managed principally by the Bureau of Land Management), but much more—and often the best—lies in private hands. This creates a situation (and not just with pronghorns) in which a public wildlife resource occupies and lives off the fat of land owned by individuals. Although there are plenty of exceptions, most western ranchers like wildlife on their land and do not begrudge pronghorns and their wild brethren the forage they consume, as long as the rancher's bottom line is not affected too adversely. It follows, therefore, that people who appreciate a prairie dotted with antelope owe a debt of gratitude to the private ranchers who provide these animals' room and board. The next time the opportunity arises, you might consider thanking a rancher for giving antelope a home.

Antelope Enemies

IN A VERY REAL, but very long-term, predators made antelope the prairie speedsters they are today. In the wild world, physical attributes don't just happen, they are slowly selected for generation after generation by the individuals that survive. Today's antelope run like the wind because some of their ancestors were able to outdistance the carnivores that would have made a meal of them (or at least they outdistanced one of their herdmates, that slower fellow who produced no descendants).

Had all predators in North America's dawning days been slow and sluggish, pronghorns today might be no faster than

a cow. But in those distant times at least some of the many carnivores earned their livings not primarily by stealth or cunning but by speed or endurance. For uncounted generations, these fleet eaters of meat pursued the pronghorns and killed enough of the slower ones so that the others learned to run as if their lives depended on it (which they did).

Although many predators probably helped spur antelope on to athletic greatness, it was likely an American version of the cheetah (an animal called *Felix trumani*) and a long-legged hyena-like creature *(Chasmaporthetes)* that supplied much of the pressure. These predators have since passed

Snarling gray wolf, a pronghorn predator, Montana

from the scene, but the memory of their lightning pursuit still lingers deep in the collective pronghorn brain. The band of antelope that races today at breakneck speed across the prairie is really running from these two and their kin, not from the snail-paced human, or even the coyote, left coughing in their dust.

In more recent millennia, virtually every large predator species on the continent has at one time or another killed antelope. Grizzlies and cougars used to live on the plains, and they no doubt dined occasionally (perhaps even often) on pronghorn steaks. Bobcats have been known to do the same, and perhaps even a badger or fox is now and then able to snatch an unattended newborn fawn. Bears and cougars, however, long ago ceased sharing much habitat with antelope, having been forced by human persecution to live mostly in inaccessible mountainous terrain. Likewise, the smaller carnivores, though rather capable predators for their size, would be little match for a protective doe antelope.

This, for the most part, has left antelope predation to the two acknowledged masters of canine expertise—wolves and coyotes. Once, gray wolves cruised the prairie in countless packs, preying on whatever large animals they encountered. Often, this meant bison, but plenty of ante-

lope probably found their way into wolf stomachs as well. Wolves kill antelope the way they dispatch all their prey— in pieces. These efficient predators are team players, complete with a leader/coach to make the decisions.

Often, the wolves' modus operandi entailed stalking as closely as possible to a feeding herd, then rushing the startled antelope. With luck (good luck for the wolves, bad luck for the antelope), an individual pronghorn would stand out at the edge of the fleeing herd by being slower, weaker, older, younger, or in some other way more vulnerable. Or perhaps this individual would simply choose, for whatever reason, to break from the ranks and strike an escape route of its own. If just one wolf was able to sink its teeth into a hind leg of this antelope, the outcome was probably decided. In a few seconds, other members of the pack would arrive to bite and tear at other parts of the antelope's anatomy. Soon, the prey would go down, and the engorgement of wolf bellies would begin. Meanwhile, the rest of the antelope herd might watch from a distant ridge.

For countless generations, wolves probably got a fair percentage of their sustenance from pronghorns, especially in the spring when the extremely vulnerable fawns were plentiful. Nature, of course, tended to keep these (and many other) species in balance—never so many wolves that pronghorn prosperity was threatened, and never so few that antelope overpopulated their range. It was a good system, and one that might have gone on forever had modern humans not appeared on the scene.

During the last part of the nineteenth century and the first part of the twentieth, Caucasian settlers arrived in great numbers on the western range and promptly disrupted the antelope-wolf equation. With singular dedication, people persecuted wolves, because of the taste these carnivores acquired for beef and mutton and because of irrational fears about potential attacks on humans. As the wolf retreated before the human juggernaut, the coyote's stock began to climb. Once held in check by its larger cousin, the coyote was now free to expand both its range and its numbers. In short order, these song dogs became the primary predators of pronghorns. Sometimes, certainly, they employed—and probably still employ—the pack attack techniques patented by wolves.

Naturalist George Bird Grinnell once witnessed an impressive display of coyote teamwork. From atop a small butte, he saw a single coyote pursuing a pronghorn doe. The antelope's normally swift pace had declined to a lope, and the coyote's tongue drooped from its mouth, leading

Grinnell to guess that the chase had been in progress for some time. Still, there probably was little chance of the coyote overtaking the doe. "Suddenly," Grinnell later wrote, "almost at the heels of the antelope, appeared a second coyote, which now took up the running, while the one that had been chasing her sat down." Into the distance the pair ran, but the antelope bore steadily to its left, in effect traveling in a large circle. Watching all this, the resting coyote trotted off some two hundred yards to where it appeared the antelope might next pass. There the refreshed predator hid in the grass. As Grinnell watched, the weary antelope approached, now with two coyotes on her trail, one quite close and the other farther back. Apparently, a third pursuer had taken over the chase from the second. As the pronghorn neared the hiding coyote, the predator repeatedly peeked above the grass to gauge the doe's precise route, then crawled on its belly to get into a better position to intercept her. "When the antelope reached the place where the coyote lay hidden, he sprang up and in a jump or two caught her neck and threw her down," wrote Grinnell. In a moment, the other two predators arrived to join in the feast.

Most coyotes, however, hunt singly or in pairs, and most antelope don't get caught alone on the prairie.

Consequently, coyotes do not constitute a major threat to adult antelope. On plenty of occasions, in fact, it is the predator and not the intended prey that comes up the loser in a coyote-pronghorn confrontation.

Fawns are a different story, however. Young antelope are left alone by their grazing mothers for much of the day for the first several weeks of life, and during this time have no real defense against predators—other than hiding, which they happen to do very well. So any coyote or other predator that can locate a young fawn may well have an easy meal (provided the angry doe doesn't show up). Consequently, coyotes and other carnivores can wreak havoc on fawns, sometimes destroying most of a year's crop. The amount of fawn predation in a given area depends on several factors, including predator density, available cover, and the abundance or scarcity of alternative prey.

Not every antelope predator has its feet planted on the ground. Now and then a golden eagle swoops down out of the western sky to take a pronghorn life. Biologists believe such incidents to be fairly rare, but on several occasions trained observers have witnessed the event. Just after dawn one December morning near Laramie, Wyoming, Gregory Goodwin watched a golden eagle attack a male pronghorn fawn. As the antelope (part of a large herd) grazed on the

side of a small rise, the raptor came over the hill about thirty feet above the ground. It hit the fawn in the back, and both animals tumbled to the ground. The herd raced off, and the wounded and stunned fawn straggled after it. When the young antelope had gone half a mile, the eagle hit it again, but once more the fawn righted itself and fled. At the third strike, the eagle remained atop the antelope's back, spreading its wings for balance as the terrified fawn ran in circles. A moment later, the fawn collapsed and died soon after.

Eldon Bruns, a biologist at the University of Calgary, witnessed a similar event on the Alberta prairie: A golden eagle flew over a pronghorn herd and landed on a rock barely fifty yards away. Immediately, the antelope rose from their scattered resting locations and formed a tight clump facing the bird. It was apparent that the pronghorns considered the raptor a very real threat. For two minutes the staring match continued. Then the eagle took off and flew directly at the herd. Three pronghorns in the front of the group advanced a few steps toward the oncoming raptor and made pawing motions in the air with their front legs. Then the entire herd turned and ran, still in a tight group.

Twice the eagle stooped toward the rearmost members of the herd, but both times failed to make contact. On the third try, however, its talons caught a female fawn squarely

on the back. By running and jumping, the fawn was able to dislodge the bird, but on its next dive the predator caught another young antelope. For a few minutes, the fawn bucked and tried to shake its enemy loose, but the eagle, mounted at a right angle to the antelope's length, hung on tenaciously, frequently spreading its wings for balance. Soon, the fawn stumbled, and moments later it died. Bruns attributed its death to shock and exhaustion. In other instances, eagles have been known to kill large prey by using their rapierlike talons to puncture an artery or sever nerves.

Gruesome as incidents like these may sound, they are part of the natural order. In and of themselves, predators are neither good nor evil, for those terms are human inventions. Coyotes, eagles, and other meat-eaters kill so that they—and their offspring—may live. Too many antelope and the forage would disappear and starvation follow. Too many predators and the antelope would vanish, leaving the coyotes with less to eat. It is an ageless balancing act.

Coyote stalking prey, Alberta, Canada

CHAPTER NINE

Fighting Back

IN HIS BOOK *The Pronghorn Antelope and Its Management*, Arthur Einarsen describes a drama he witnessed in southern Oregon:

A lone coyote hunted a broad basin, crisscrossing the area and frequently testing the wind for smells of potential food. Suddenly, the predator caught the scent of an antelope fawn hiding some considerable distance upwind. The coyote moved to the attack, using its nose as its sole guide and frequently ranging sideways to once again pick up the scent it seemed to lose from time to time. When it had closed to within one hundred yards or so, the coyote apparently spotted the fawn's

hiding place and began a crouching stalk that before long brought it within fifteen feet of its prey.

All this, however, did not escape the attention of two pronghorn does—one apparently the fawn's mother—grazing on the basin rim some distance away. As the predator closed in on the fawn, says Einarsen, the two does "broke away from the rim, and running neck and neck thundered down the slope, both heading straight as an arrow for the skulking coyote." At the last moment, the coyote noticed its attackers and leaped aside, barely avoiding their wrath—and their hooves. Pressing the assault, both does flailed away

Pronghorn buck displaying flared rump patch, Montana

at the coyote with their front feet, quickly convincing the predator that it was not so hungry after all. Terrified, the coyote headed posthaste for the safety of some rimrocks half a mile away, covering much of that distance with an angry antelope only a step or two behind. Moments later, the fawn was back in hiding, and the does had resumed feeding.

Though not usually thought of as aggressive or very adept at active defense, pronghorns are capable of inflicting considerable physical harm on an adversary. Their hooves are hard and pointed, their legs strong, and the tips of their horns (especially in mature bucks) sharp. Bucks battling for mating rights have been known to kill each other with a well-placed horn thrust, and it is certainly possible that they might do the same to a predator. Does protecting their young are most likely to become attacker antelope, but now and then bucks also have been known to forcefully evict coyotes from the premises.

In his book *The World of the Pronghorn*, Joe Van Wormer tells of driving a back road one day and coming upon a menacing looking pronghorn doe that appeared ready to attack his car. Then he spotted a coyote peeking sheepishly from a nearby metal culvert, where it apparently had been chased by the antelope, which now stood guard over the predator. At Van Wormer's arrival, the coyote bolted from the far end of the culvert, but instantly the doe gave chase, and the canine returned ignominiously to the safety of the tunnel. A moment later, the coyote—apparently fearing the human more than the doe—attempted another escape, and in the process barely avoided disaster by moving at the last possible second as the doe landed with all four feet on the spot the coyote had just vacated. With the antelope temporarily off balance, the coyote broke for the nearby brush, where it managed to elude its enemy. As the predator ran, Van Wormer noticed its pronounced limp, quite possibly the result of the original antelope assault that had sent it scurrying for cover.

In addition to a sometimes irascible personality (particularly in mothering does), antelope employ several defenses to help keep them from becoming a predator's next meal. Foremost among these, of course, is speed, the very hallmark of the species. The theory is utter simplicity: Run away from danger faster than danger can run after you. When you're as fast as a pronghorn, speed works almost every time, which is why these animals have survived so well for twenty million year or so. (Antelope fleetness afoot is covered in chapter 4.)

When you're running a race, especially one that is a matter of your own life and death, a head start is always nice, and antelope usually get a good one. Thanks to some of the best eyesight this side of Superman's x-ray vision, antelope rarely allow any enemy to get very close before they launch a pell-mell rush toward safer pastures. Because no pronghorn has ever cooperated with an optometrist to have its vision checked and quantified, we must rely mostly on guesswork and anecdotal evidence to determine how well these creatures see. Liver-eating Johnson—that famous mountain man, trapper, scout, and basis for the character played by Robert Redford in the movie *Jeremiah Johnson*—is reported to have commented thus on pronghorn visual acuity:

> *What alive antelope don't see between dawn and dark isn't visible from his standpoint; and while you're a-gawkin' at him through that there glass to make out whether he's a rock or a goat, he's a-countin' your cartridges and makin' up his mind which way he'll scoot when you disappear in the draw for to sneak on him—and don't you ferget it.*

For decades, a dictum floating around the antelope hunting fraternity has said that pronghorn vision is equal to that of a person looking through eight-power binoculars (binoculars that magnify things to eight times their actual size). No one knows for sure, but this comparison probably originated on the typewriter keys of someone writing for the sporting magazines, someone whose attempts at antelope stalking more often than not ended in being detected long before getting into rifle range. Whether antelope eyes are the equivalent of eight-power magnification or four-power or even ten-power is anyone's guess, but many hunters do feel outgunned visually by pronghorns unless they (the hunters) are looking through binoculars, most of which are seven-power or eight-power.

Another way to look at antelope eyesight is to see what catches their eye, then determine how far away that thing is. Anyone who spends any time at all watching antelope is likely to see them go from a placid resting or feeding mode to instant alert for no apparent reason. The entire herd may stare in one direction, but still the human cannot understand why. Then, with the aid of binoculars, the observer sees that a hunter (or a truck, a pair of coyotes, or some other perceived threat) has just popped into view three ridges distant. Einarsen says quite matter-of-factly that moving objects three or four miles away can attract an antelope's

attention. That may be a bit of an exaggeration, but lots of hunters have had the experience of scanning the prairie a mile or two away with binoculars only to spot a pronghorn already staring back at him.

Powerful though they may be, pronghorn peepers do have shortcomings. Like many animals, antelope spot unusual movement much more quickly than unusual shapes. For example, a person moving across the prairie a mile (or more) away is likely to set off antelope alarms far sooner than one sitting rock-still in plain view at only a fraction of that distance. One early naturalist put it this way: "[The antelope] cannot readily tell a horse from a buffalo or a man from a bush, if they are perfectly still, unless they are quite near." Indeed, many a hunter has had the experience—simultaneously rewarding and frustrating—of plodding all day across the prairie with the antelope always a mile away only to have one or more of the animals walk within easy range while he or she sits quietly resting.

Popular pronghorn literature is replete with references to another pronghorn idiosyncrasy that seems to fly in the face of the animal's reputation for wariness. This involves

Close-up of pronghorn buck, Montana

a hunting technique, called tolling, that is supposed to work like this: Either by stalking or sitting tight and letting the antelope approach him or her, the hunter gets within a few hundred yards of a herd without being detected. Then, instead of remaining hidden, the hunter raises an arm and slowly waves back and forth a handkerchief, hat, or other item. In a pinch, a hand alone will do. Some accounts even have the hunter lying on his back and slowly churning his legs in the air. The keen-eyed pronghorns, of course, note these unusual goings-on and—curious to a fault—come to investigate. Once they amble within range, the hunter shoots. At least that's the theory.

Few hunters today try tolling antelope, and perhaps for good reason. For most sportsmen, tolling is probably a waste of time, more likely to send antelope into the next county than to lure them within range. So, were all those old accounts of successful tolling the result of wishful thinking or overactive imaginations? Maybe. It is also possible, however, that decades ago when far fewer people ventured onto the prairie and fewer still hunted antelope, pronghorns could indeed be tolled. But as contacts with humans (and the attendant plethora of odd sights) became almost a common occurrence for antelope, it could be that they either lost their curiosity or learned that strange stuff on the open prairie usually spelled trouble.

Aside from visual alertness and speed, each individual antelope's best defense is its social nature. Different wildlife species live in groups for various reasons. Hunting in packs allows wolves to kill larger prey. Some birds hang out together because if one finds food, they'll all eat. The high sociability of prairie dogs puts more eyes on the lookout for predators. Antelope, too, employ this "many eyes" defense. While some lower their heads to feed, others look about for danger, and in this way the herd is never without sentinels.

Pronghorn sociability, however, likely has more to do with competition than with cooperation. Although an individual antelope might indeed benefit from its neighbor's vigilance, a better reason for having others of its kind around is to have someone to sacrifice. In nature's survival-is-everything world, staying alive is the only thing that really matters, even if that success comes at the expense of another member of the group. Canadian wildlife biologist and behavioral researcher Valerius Geist puts it this way: "The chap in the middle of the herd is always safe, and those on the edge need only to run faster than their slowest herdmate." So it is that when antelope flee an attacker, they are running

not so much to outdistance the predator as to outdistance at least one other antelope. It may sound cruel, but this is the way the wild world works.

There is one more kind of defense that may be at work in protecting running antelope. It is little more than a theory, but it might help explain the distinctive white-on-brown striped pattern of pronghorn pelage. The idea suggested here is that when a herd of antelope runs tightly bunched across the uneven prairie, the movement of their contrasting colors has a kind of hypnotic effect on predators. According to this speculation, the undulating color pattern helps blend the many antelope into one throbbing entity that supposedly stymies, though perhaps just momentarily, the predator's quest for a specific individual to attack. A century-and-a-half ago, an astute John James Audubon described the effect like this:

> They [pronghorns] pass along, up or down hills or along the level plains with the same apparent ease, while so rapidly do their legs perform their graceful movements in propelling their bodies over the ground, that, like the spokes of a fast turning wheel, we can hardly see them, but instead observe a gauzy or film-like appearance where they should be visible.

Now, this notion may seem like the imaginative wanderings of a naturalist with too little to do, but some research biologists believe there may be something to it. The effect probably would be most pronounced with the mesmerizing stripes of Africa's zebras, but pronghorns could also be capable of dazzling a predator this way. Keep in mind that the difference between a successful escape and a dead antelope might well come down to a mere second's hesitation or indecision on the predator's part. So, any additional advantage could indeed be a matter of life and death. If you cannot detect any blurring or hypnotic effect while watching running antelope with your own eyes, remember that a predator would, like the antelope, be running full bore amid the dust and uncertainty of the prairie. From that perspective, things might look rather different. Researchers on horseback who have pursued running pronghorns report that it is nearly impossible to keep track of an individual antelope when the fleeing herd makes a sharp turn. And it is by focusing on an individual that predators succeed.

Another defensive technique is most definitely tied to the pronghorn's unique color scheme. The rounded contours of the animal's rump, constituting a fairly large portion of its total torso, is brilliantly, blatantly white. Not cream or buff or tan, but pure white. Just as white-tailed deer use their flaglike tails to signal alarm, antelope flare their rump patches to alert herdmates to danger. Special muscles just under the skin facilitate the instantaneous raising or lowering of each individual rump hair, and at the first sign of danger, that rear end can fairly scream a warning to herdmates—and to distant herds. Fawns only a few days out of the womb can perform this signaling maneuver.

Flared to its fullest, a brilliant pronghorn rump resembles nothing so much as a dazzling white chrysanthemum. On a bright day, a few sparkling white antelope derrieres can have the same attention-getting effect as mirrors flashing in the sunlight. Humans like to think that their inventions—smoke puffs, hoisted flags, semaphore signals, and others—constituted the first long-distance communication. Not so. Pronghorns beat them to it by several million years.

What it all comes down to is that pronghorns can generally take care of themselves. They have outlived competitors and predators alike not by being victims, but by being survivors. At each threatening juncture—the appearance of a new predator or a great climatic change, for examples—they have evolved fresh techniques to help them cope, to keep the species alive. Great speed, keen eyes, communication, social living—these and other defenses have combined to create the best offense of all, survivability.

Kidding Around

ASIDE FROM THE MACHINATIONS of the rut, perhaps the most interesting pronghorn goings-on involve fawns—and the action starts early. Typically, a sexually mature doe produces from four to seven (sometimes as many as nine) eggs for possible fertilization during the breeding season. Since she will probably give birth to twins (except for her first pregnancy, which usually produces a single fawn), it might be expected that two of these ova would be fertilized while the extras are sloughed off. Not so. According to biologist Bart O'Gara, a long-time wildlife researcher at the University of

Montana, a microscopic struggle for survival goes on within the womb.

Frequently, all available eggs become fertilized, with the resulting blastocysts then engaging in an intrauterine battle to see which pair will survive. While still threadlike in shape, these tiny embryos float freely about the uterus. Some become tangled and knotted and eventually die of malnutrition. A month after being fertilized, the surviving embryos (often as many as four) attach themselves to the uterine wall. Invariably, two of these receive the lion's share of nutrients, allowing them to grow faster than the others. As they do,

Pronghorn doe with fawns, one nursing, Montana

projections emerging from their embryonic sheaths may puncture the others and kill them. Or embryos receiving too few nutrients may simply wither and die. The two survivors of this intrauterine competition become the twins that the doe will, in about eight months, present to the world.

Sometime in late winter or spring (as early as February in the South and as late as June in the North), the pregnant doe purposefully falls behind the grazing herd to select a site for dropping her fawns. Although pronghorn births are not synchronized—like those of caribou, for example—to occur in massive numbers simultaneously (to preclude predators picking off the newborns one-by-one over a longer period), most of a herd's fawns tend to show up during the same period of a few weeks.

After an hour or more of nervous and peripatetic anticipation, the doe lies on her side and with a rocking motion starts her offspring's entry into the world. Typically, the white tips of the front hooves constitute the first sign of the emerging newborn. Minutes later, the doe may stand to allow the youngster to slide free. In less than half an hour, the neonate is usually joined by a twin, although the second fawn may be dropped some distance from the first. At birth, each newcomer is likely to weigh between five and

seven pounds. The doe licks the fawns dry and consumes the afterbirth (presumably to prevent it from attracting predators). Soon, the newborns take their first nourishment.

At birth, pronghorn fawns lack the striking and distinctive coloration of their parents. They are instead a nondescript grayish brown, and the rump patch that will one day flare brilliantly white is for now a subdued yellow. Their hair ripples across their small bodies in curly waves.

Barely an hour after its birth, the fawn—on its own but under the doe's supervision—selects a bedding site and lies down, usually a short distance away from the birthing site to separate it from any odors that may linger. The twin, if there is one, does likewise somewhere nearby. By hiding her fawns in separate locations, a doe reduces the chances that a predator will kill both youngsters. To help foil predators even more, fawns may change their bedding sites several times per day.

Every five hours or so, the doe returns from grazing to check on her offspring, feed them, and give the fawns a chance to stretch their legs. To human eyes, it may seem that the doe is, for the most part, abandoning her fawns, but in

Pronghorn fawn in western Montana, hiding

reality she is increasing their chances of survival by keeping them hidden away from the herd. Adult antelope are prominent sights on the prairie, and if newborns bedded with the herd, it would be easy for predators to find and kill them.

For the next three weeks the youngsters will spend most of their time lying motionless in these spots while their mother is away. When at ease, a bedded fawn is likely to lie curled on its belly with its head turned back toward its rear. Or it may lie with its head up and alert. When danger threatens, however, fawns instinctively know how to press themselves flat against the earth, perhaps with chin extended between their outstretched front legs. Rising only a few inches above the ground, totally motionless, and effectively camouflaged, they seem to disappear, becoming for the moment nothing more than a rock or lump of prairie sod.

Every antelope biologist can tell tales about the fawns he or she knew were there but could never find. In his book *The World of the Pronghorn,* Joe Van Wormer says that on one occasion three researchers pinpointed through a spotting scope the exact location of a pair of fawns a thousand yards away. They determined that the two were lying about twenty yards apart. Arriving at the spot, they soon located one of the youngsters, but the other proved more elusive. For two hours, the men methodically searched the vicinity, but to no avail. Although they likely had come within inches of stepping on the animal, they eventually had to give up the search and move on. Even pronghorn mothers sometimes have trouble finding their own fawns.

Another nifty bit of biology that helps keep pronghorn young out of coyote stomachs is the fawn's virtual absence of odor. Van Wormer describes an incident in which he and two graduate students used a pair of black Labrador retrievers to help find hiding fawns. Labs are supposed to have pretty good noses, but at one point one of the dogs strolled all around a stock-still fawn at a distance of only a few feet. Finally, the dog lay down barely a foot from the young antelope but was still ignorant of its existence. The dog simply could not smell the fawn.

Biologists sometimes quarrel about just how odor-free pronghorn youngsters actually are, since coyotes have been observed stalking bedded fawns (apparently by smell), but there seems to be little question that their relative lack of scent often saves their young lives. Certainly, lots of young fawns fall prey to predators, but the eons have proven that keeping them hidden during their early days will ensure that plenty survive to adulthood as well.

During her regular visits, up to six hours apart, the mother nurses and grooms her youngsters. She also helps keep fawn bedding areas odor-free by consuming the youngsters' feces and urine. Upon the mother's arrival at the bedding site, the fawn stands and prominently raises its rump. As the doe licks its anogenital region, the fawn empties its bladder and bowel, and the doe ingests the wastes. The mother dutifully repeats this frequent house-keeping chore until the fawns are two or three weeks of age.

As the days tick by, the fawns become increasingly restless in their perpetual hiding places. By the age of three weeks or so, the youngsters may start punctuating their isolation with lots of movement—getting up, lying down, turning around, grooming, scratching with a hind foot, strolling about, and pawing the ground. About this time (perhaps sensing the futility of further isolation), the doe brings her youngsters out of hiding and into the herd. As other mothers do likewise, small nursery bands form.

With lots of youngsters scampering about, it's important for a doe to recognize her own offspring (and vice versa), and it appears that much of this identification is accomplished visually, although smell is often the clincher. In some circumstances, fawns also may recognize their mother's voice. Some observers have reported something akin to antelope day care, nursery bands where does tend their own fawns and other of the herd's young. Although the fre-quency of this behavior has probably been exaggerated, does have been known to nurse fawns whose mothers had died.

As soon as the fawn has been liberated from its mother's womb, perhaps even before it hits the ground, there begins an amazing exhibition of precociousness. Imagine for a moment a human newborn with its complete dependence on adults and its inability for many months to perform normal tasks such as walking, talking, self-feeding, obedience, and staying out of harm's way. Now consider the pronghorn infant: Barely twenty minutes into the world, the fawn may be on its feet searching for the doe's udder. Within thirty minutes of birth, the youngster takes its first steps. At four days of age, it can outrun a man. A week later, the fawn can keep up with its mother and run up to three miles without tiring. After three weeks, it eats vegetation. In three months, it acquires the striking pelage of its parents, including the bright white rump patch. By the age of seven months, a fawn weighs about sixty pounds, more than half of its eventual total weight of one hundred pounds or so.

One reason for the fawn's rapid maturation is the relatively long time it spends in the womb—about 252 days. This is a longer gestation than that of several larger animals, including deer (196 days), bighorn sheep (180 days), and mountain goats (160 days). Another reason is

Robert Campbell

Pronghorn fawn in western Montana, nursing

the high-quality food it gets. Consuming forage that no self-respecting bovine would even touch, a lactating pronghorn doe creates some of the richest milk in nature, with twice the protein and more than three times the fat of cow's milk. "The [antelope] mother's milk is as thick as undiluted evaporated milk, but less sweet," wrote naturalist John James Audubon, who apparently had tasted the liquid. Fawns continue to nurse until they are about four months old.

Though fawnhood, with the almost constant threat of predators, is a dangerous time, antelope young seem to find plenty of time for play. Arthur Einarsen, author of *The Pronghorn Antelope and Its Management*, relates this scene, which he observed in the Spanish Lake area of southern Oregon:

The mothers were contentedly resting in the warm June sun, and the fawns were having a great time in a highly organized game. Rushing away across the flat rim of the lakeshore, as though started by a lifting of a barrier on a race track, they ran neck and neck, swung in a wide arc and then thundered back, their tiny hoofs beating in unison as they soared rather than ran, their bodies parallel to the earth. Upon nearing the starting point they drew up to a stiff-legged stop at their mothers' sides, gazed with dreamy eyes around the immediate vicinity, then wheeled away on another flight, with apparently enough power and enthusiasm to drive them to the summit of the Rocky Mountains a thousand miles away.

They swung in a wide arc and raced back to the point of beginning. One of the fawns in exuberance leaped upon his mother's back as she lay resting and stood there with distended nostrils sucking in the desert air and beaming contentment. With a toss of his head he leaped off and landed on the back of another doe. Only an occasional twitch of the skin by the adults showed their mild displeasure. Evidently all was well, so two other fawns followed suit. Soon there was a wild round of leaping and bounding, and a game of tag was in full swing with the does as bases. The young bounded from back to back with little spurts to eat up the distance between mothers.

At the National Bison Range in Montana, biologist John Byers put pronghorn play under the scientific microscope. It begins, he says, as early as the second day after birth and reaches its peak three or four weeks later when most of the herd's newborns have emerged from hiding to become part of pronghorn society. Typically, a fawn suckles, stands dazed for a few moments, fidgets, then launches into

Woman feeding antelope fawn

James Tallon

97

some sort of running, jumping, bounding, kicking, pirouetting activity. Since does in a herd tend to nurse their young about the same time, recreating fawns often have playmates, and the sight of several fawns gamboling as if there were no tomorrow can be eminently entertaining for any human lucky enough to witness the event. Between spurts of frolicking, fawns may head back to the milk bar for refreshments or, in Byers' words, "Simply stand there looking expectant, as though they don't quite understand what's happening to them."

After these preliminaries come the kind of main running events that Einarsen described. At the age of twenty-five days, a fawn's demonstration of speed may last only a minute or two, although these youngsters are capable of races that last up to five minutes. The whole episode is often capped off with an exhibition of stotting, a gait in which all four legs leave (and return to) the ground at the same time—sort of like running in place on four pogo sticks. Finally, the little athletes stand still and pant.

Most of this strenuous activity, says Byers, is intended to prepare fawns for the high-speed running that may one day

keep them from becoming a predator's dinner. In addition to getting young legs in shape, however, play activities help prepare fawns for the hierarchical society of the herd. Fawns (usually the males) sometimes pick mock fights with one another, lowering their heads and engaging in little pushing battles like pairs of diminutive wrestlers. Occasionally, one fawn will mount another, although they are incapable of any sexual activity. Even female fawns, however, engage in some pushing and shoving, actions that may be the early signs of the dominance ranking that helps keep order in the herd.

At the age of four or five months, male fawns often break the bonds with their mothers and join the bachelor herds. Female youngsters, because they are tolerated by territorial bucks, may stay with their mothers throughout the summer and into the fall. A few of these young does may breed during their first autumn, but most will wait another year to begin producing their own fawns.

Pronghorn buck with doe, Montana

CHAPTER ELEVEN

Don't Fence Me In

WHEN THE POET Robert Frost wrote that good fences make good neighbors, he wasn't talking about antelope. Fences give pronghorns fits. Four feet of mesh fencing that deer would scarcely notice can radically affect the lives of antelope by keeping them from watering holes, putting feeding areas off limits, and blocking traditional migration routes. There are even reports of coyotes maneuvering pronghorn prey into fence corners where they become easy victims. Fences simply are anathema to antelope.

The reason is simple: Antelope don't jump. And why should they? Antelope evolved on the prairie eons ago, and

for millions of years there was nothing vertical for them to jump over. Rocks and bushes were about the only things in their environment with any height, and invariably it proved a whole lot easier to go around instead of over these obstacles. As antelope genes were passed down over countless generations, any original jumping inclination that might have existed gradually disappeared.

By comparison, white-tailed deer evolved in the forest, where going around every fallen log would make any escape extremely slow and probably unsuccessful. So, white-tails became leapers of great renown, capable of clearing vertical

Young pronghorn running along fence line

(Photograph by Robert Winslow)

barriers several feet high. As many gardeners in white-tail habitat can tell you, it usually takes more than a six-foot fence to keep deer out of the cabbage patch. But not antelope. The most meager of fences can make prisoners of pronghorns.

It's not that antelope don't have the proper jumping equipment. They are, after all, some of the best animal athletes in the world. Their legs are well muscled and perfectly capable of clearing tall fences in a single bound. They don't hesitate to make significant horizontal leaps (reportedly up to twenty-five feet) over such features as small draws and wet areas. Many also are able to make the lateral leap necessary to carry them over a cattle guard. (Also called a Texas gate, this device consists of a series of parallel wood or metal beams set close together at ground level in the position of a gate in a fence. Cattle refuse to cross the gapped beams, but vehicles can drive over without having to open a gate.)

On rare occasions, antelope do choose to go over something vertical. In one incident in Texas, ten captive antelope reportedly escaped their enclosure by jumping over a five-foot mesh fence. When reincarcerated, these animals cleared the fence a second time, despite the extra six inches that had been added to its height. On another occasion, antelope reportedly jumped an eight-foot barrier. Biologist Bart O'Gara tells of one doe at an Oregon capture site that attempted to escape by leaping over a fifteen-foot rock wall, a feat he says she nearly accomplished.

Once, a Nevada pronghorn was observed leaping—vertically—over little more than his imagination. Traveling the back country one day, Stanley Jewett (who later reported the incident in the *Journal of Mammalogy*) came upon an antelope buck standing in the middle of the road. At Jewett's approach, the buck began running down the road, but every few yards the animal leaped high into the air. Again and again. Run and leap. Run and leap. Finally, Jewett figured things out. A line of telephone poles paralleled the route, and the afternoon sun caused their shadows to fall across the road. Every time the buck came to a shadow in his path, he perceived it as something to be hurdled, which he did for more than a mile.

When they do jump, pronghorns seem to accomplish the feat with poise, leading some observers to compare their leaping to the effortless white-tail style of jumping. Wilf Pyle, co-author of *The Hunter's Book of the Pronghorn Antelope*, once came upon a big buck on a remote back road. "When that buck realized that a car was approaching," he writes, "he took two short steps and easily cleared the three-strand fence . . . with a grace and ease that would have led a casual observer to think pronghorns are habitual jumpers."

No, it's not that antelope can't jump vertically—it's that (with rare exceptions) they simply won't. Perhaps somewhere in the pronghorn brain lies a net of neurons that automatically interprets any vertical obstacle as incapable of being cleared. If you're an antelope, you go around vertical barriers, not over them, and you don't bother to imagine otherwise. Vertical jumping just doesn't compute. You might as well ask these animals to read a few lines from Shakespeare. Other theorists have suggested that the exceptionally sharp (and perhaps far-sighted) pronghorn eyes cannot focus properly on a close fence or cannot gauge its (virtually nonexistent) depth. Who knows?

None of this was a problem, of course, until sheep and cattle ranchers began showing up in great numbers on the plains. Then, gradually, the wide-open prairie got subdivided into increasingly smaller plots of ownership, each of which typically ended up with a fence around it. And within it, as individual ranchers further chopped their own holdings into pastures. Unlike some problems that antelope faced, such as uncontrolled market hunting, fences could not be legislated away or ameliorated by wise game management, and they remain a significant impediment in some areas today.

Antelope cope with fences in various ways, depending on the kind of barrier involved. Easiest for them to handle is the three-strand, barbed-wire fence designed to keep cattle (but not sheep) from straying. If the bottom strand is far enough above the ground (at least seventeen inches or so), antelope can usually go under it. Typically, a running pronghorn approaching such a fence drops to its knees, folds the front legs back beneath the body, puts its chest on the ground, arches the shoulders downward, and pushes forward with the hind legs until it's possible to stand up on the other side. Pronghorns become so adept at this maneuver that slow-motion video is required to identify all the steps involved. When pressed by hunters or predators, they are able to accomplish the moves with an absolutely minimal loss of speed.

Going under any fence (especially a low-strung one and especially when the animal is in a hurry) can take a toll, however. Frequently, patches of hair from antelope backs cling to the wire where pronghorns have crossed, and otherwise healthy animals killed by hunters often carry scars and/or hairless spots on their backs. Now and then, ranchers find the decaying remains of a pronghorn with a leg entangled in fence wire. In many locales, antelope quickly find the best places to scoot under fences, usually spots where erosion, a dry streambed, or something

Robert Campbell

Pronghorn buck climbing under barbed-wire fence, Colorado

else has formed a small trench beneath the fence and therefore increased the distance between the ground and the bottom wire.

A four-strand, barbed-wire fence makes things tougher, since the lowest strand is likely to be closer to the ground. When chased hard—and apparently aware that crawling under is not on the agenda—antelope have been known to blast through fences of this type at full speed, breaking wires and leaving a cloud of hair floating on the breeze.

The worst kind of fence, from an antelope's point of view, is the woven wire mesh type used for sheep. If a pronghorn can penetrate one of these fences, it's likely a woolly could, too, and so these obstructions are almost by definition antelope-proof except for the occasional scooting-under spots that may develop. In some instances, sheep-proof fences have denied antelope access to crucial habitat and have left them starving along the fence lines.

Ironically, antelope may become so conditioned to the existence of a fence that they fail to notice its absence. More than once, ranchers or wildlife officials have laid down portions of fences to facilitate antelope crossings only to have the antelope continue to react as if the barrier were still intact. It seems that once they get used to a fence being in a certain place, it may be difficult to disabuse them of that notion. Often, however, they do learn to travel through gates that remain open most of the time.

Some management agencies have even tried building ramps to get pronghorns over fences. Typically, such a construction might consist of a dirt runway a dozen feet wide that begins at sod level several feet from the fence and rises to a height of thirty inches or so at its peak three feet from the fence. A mirror-image ramp is built on the opposite side of the wire. Since antelope are good broad jumpers, the theory is that they will climb the ramp, make the mostly horizontal leap over the fence, and glide down the ramp on the far side. Perhaps some antelope became adept at this new athletic event, but ramps never caught on—maybe because they are rather costly to build, especially in the remote places where they might be most needed.

The most egregious example of fences inhibiting antelope movements occurred in the early 1980s in the Red Rim area southwest of Rawlins, Wyoming. The Red Rim contains about thirty-five square miles of prime antelope winter range, high plains blown free of snow where pronghorns can find food as well as gullies to protect them from the worst of the winds. About half this land was public

ground (managed by federal and state agencies) and half privately held by rancher Taylor Lawrence, who also controlled the grazing rights to much of the public land. All of this terrain had been declared "critical" antelope winter habitat by the Wyoming Game and Fish Department.

In 1983, Lawrence set about building a gigantic fence to keep pronghorns off much of Red Rim. He claimed that the wintering antelope were chowing down on crested wheatgrass that rightfully belonged in the bellies of his cattle, but many observers sensed another motive. The bounty of coal that lay beneath Lawrence's land belonged to the Rocky Mountain Energy Company, and conservationists believed that Lawrence wanted to lease the land's surface rights to that firm. Since strip mining would destroy pronghorn habitat, the state would likely not allow such a project. Lawrence's apparent thinking was that if the pronghorns couldn't get to their wintering grounds on Red Rim, then the land would lose its critical habitat status, and the coal development might proceed.

So Lawrence erected twenty-eight miles of five-foot woven wire fence (at an estimated cost of 150 thousand dollars) to lock the antelope out. Although the fence was built entirely on private ground, it also prohibited the ante-

James Tallon

lope from using more than a hundred thousand acres of public land. (This is possible because ownership followed the classic western checkerboard pattern. The checkerboard, in which public and private land alternate mile by mile, was created in the last century when the federal government gave every other section to the railroads for pushing tracks across the West. The rail companies later sold much of their holdings to various buyers.)

That fall, migrating pronghorns massed along the fence, and it wasn't long before they started dying. When dead and dying antelope appeared on national television, the pressure on Lawrence escalated, and he agreed to a compromise of sorts. For the next two years, Wyoming wildlife workers were allowed to remove eight miles of fence in the winter and replace it the following spring.

Then in 1985, the National Wildlife Federation sued Lawrence in federal court, and the judge ordered the rancher to modify the fence or remove it entirely. Lawrence altered the barrier to give pronghorns room to scoot under, but appealed the ruling to the U.S. Supreme Court. When the high court declined to hear the case, the "modify or

Pronghorn herd crawling under fence, one at a time

remove" order remained in effect. In the spring of 1991, the state of Wyoming purchased the ranch, thereby ensuring pronghorns the right to winter on Red Rim in peace.

Could the antelope's bitter battle with fences be ending? Lifesaving wildlife behaviors evolve over time as the individuals that exhibit them live to reproduce in greater numbers than the individuals without the trait. For example, today's pronghorns are the fastest things on the prairie because their long-ago ancestors outran predators and lived to reproduce. The bloodlines of slower individuals ended up in wolf bellies. Well, jumping ability may work the same way.

If the individual antelope that somehow learn to jump fences stand a better chance of surviving (by getting to better food or winter range, for example), they may pass that jumping prowess on to their progeny. Eventually, the inability to jump could disappear from the antelope gene pool the same way slowness in pronghorns disappeared. Or at least that's the theory. It may take centuries to prove or disprove this notion, but some observers have noted that the number of fence-jumping antelope already seems greater in areas where fences have existed the longest, suggesting that the trait may be quickly assimi-lated. Other researchers say they can detect no increase in the number of fence-jumping pronghorns. Only time will tell.

Combating the Cold

AUTUMN IS THE APEX of the antelope year. For months the weather has been warm and the food abundant. The animals are sleek and fit and strong. The rut has passed, the fierce competition ended, and the herd's genetic heritage handed on to another generation. Following hard upon the richness of autumn, however, is—at least in northern climes—the specter of winter.

Various pronghorn groups enter winter in vastly different conditions, depending on food availability and the amount of stress and harassment the rut had entailed for them. The young of the year did not participate in breeding rituals,

and may be better off physically because of it. An adult doe's status depends somewhat on the harem she joined and whether it was ruled by a powerful territorial buck (that provided lots of protection from other males) or a novice nonterritorial master (offering minimal protection). And, of course, pregnant does have the added nutritional responsibility of nurturing one or two fetuses.

Would-be breeding bucks may have had a frustrating fall (sexually speaking) with some loss of nutritional wherewithal, but the rut is clearly hardest on the breeding bucks. For weeks, these animals have thought mostly about sex,

Pronghorn buck in Montana winter

not food, and their overall condition often shows it. With the rut ended, mature bucks may feed voraciously, and if warm weather and snowless skies linger long, they can regain most of their lost fitness. If not, they may have trouble living to greet another spring.

Antelope do not in the classic sense migrate, but the coming of winter can bring changes and movements. Now, with former mating battles forgotten, mature bucks abandon their territories to join with other bucks, does, yearlings, and fawns (now almost fully grown) to form large herds. Some of these aggregations, which may contain several hundred animals, spend the winter where they have summered, while others travel up to one hundred miles in search of a place to wait out winter. This is not necessarily a north-south movement, but rather a journey to whatever place—because of its lack of snow, superior forage, or some other factor—traditionally has made the cold season tolerable.

At first glance, pronghorns appear somewhat ill-equipped to deal with winter. Their skin is thin, their color light (and therefore less heat absorbing), and they (unlike deer and other close relatives) do not accumulate large stores of body fat. Indeed, scientists suspect that pronghorns evolved in the more southerly latitudes, then gradually extended their range northward. Along the way, they learned to cope with the sometimes incredibly harsh winters that roll across the northern plains. So, today, the antelope that will face the next blizzard to blow down from the Arctic are the descendants of generations that survived uncounted winters.

If deep snow does not keep them from finding food, antelope can wait out incredibly cold conditions, sometimes even frolicking and playing while the temperature hangs well below zero. The hair that may stand almost vertically to promote cooling during the summer lies flat in overlapping layers against the antelope's skin in winter. And inside each hair is a tiny amount of air that—collectively—provides significant insulation against the cold. In addition, wintering pronghorns have learned to avoid the biting wind by seeking out protected gullies.

In many places across antelope country, winter survival is spelled s-a-g-e-b-r-u-s-h. Often a key ingredient in pronghorn prosperity, sagebrush becomes especially important in winter when many other plants lie buried beneath the snow. Antelope are adept at using their sharp hooves to dig through snow for forage, but this consumes valuable energy that munching on taller sagebrush does not. And it is not unusual for the snow to become too deep or too crusted for digging.

Hardy though pronghorns may be, winter occasionally deals a crushing blow, as it did in South Dakota during the cold season of 1985–86. Antelope there entered winter with marginal forage on the prairie, thanks to a dry summer and some intensive livestock grazing. Then heavy snows covered whatever food did exist and alternating freezes and thaws put a crust on the snow that made pronghorn travel all but impossible. Finally, the temperatures plunged and the winds howled, sending the wind chill to nearly minus one hundred degrees Fahrenheit. The antelope held on for a while, but by spring nearly 80 percent of the state's fifty thousand or so animals had perished. (The period that followed, however, stands as a testimony to pronghorn fecundity and wise wildlife management, as the population recovered nearly all its losses in only five years.)

Around Glasgow, Montana, the winter of 1964–65 is still remembered as the time the antelope came to town. The wind that blew blizzards down from the Arctic that year brought with it more than just snow and cold. Before the advancing storm fronts came antelope by the thousands, migrating desperately from southern Saskatchewan and northern Montana into the valley of the Milk River around Glasgow. After two weeks of sustained fury, the worst of the storms broke on Christmas Day, and almost immediately authorities began getting reports about the pronghorns that had moved into town. One caller said there were 150 in a ballpark, but the responding game warden put the figure at closer to twelve hundred.

Desperate for food, the pronghorns walked the streets and sidewalks, consuming whatever shrubs and small trees they could reach. Some learned to tip over garbage cans and forage on the trash. Others were adopted by residents and fed on the back porch like family pets. Dogs killed some antelope, and others died of starvation. Some children found a macabre sort of fun in digging frozen pronghorn carcasses from the snow and standing them up like cardboard cutouts in front yards. A few people saw the invasion as an opportunity to fill their freezers, and poached antelope, perhaps even from their own front yards. Two women set up a mini antelope hospital in their garage, feeding their stronger patients livestock rations and giving the weaker ones baby cereal. They also treated the animals with vitamins from the local pharmacy.

The problems weren't just in town. Authorities who

Robert Winslow

surveyed the seventy square miles around Glasgow estimated the antelope influx at seventy-five hundred animals. Soon, ranchers began complaining that the pronghorns were eating precious hay that had been destined for cow stomachs. Like ants on an apple core, starving pronghorns swarmed around haystacks, shoving and jockeying for feeding spots, and in the process probably trampled more hay than they ate. Officials and ranchers took to fencing off the haystacks, but each time they enclosed one, the starving animals simply trudged en masse to the next—often with a fencing crew in hot pursuit. Elsewhere, weakened antelope sought refuge from the deep snow in roadways and along railroad tracks, where many of them perished in collisions.

For three-and-a-half months, the antelope made the Glasgow area their home. Finally, with spring's arrival, the exodus began, as the winter-worn animals made their way back to traditional summer ranges in northern Montana and Canada. But the losses were great. From the vicinity of the town alone, authorities hauled off 842 antelope carcasses, and they put the estimated pronghorn death toll for the region at three thousand.

Mercifully, such major calamities as those in Montana and South Dakota are rare. For the most part, antelope deal well with winter, which is something of a must for any denizen of the northern plains.

Pronghorns in snowstorm

CHAPTER THIRTEEN

The Human Predator

FOR EONS, ALL PRONGHORNS had to worry about were wolves, coyotes, cougars, and assorted other four-legged or avian predators, many of which have since passed from the scene. Although these meat eaters created considerable problems for individual antelope (by consuming them), things couldn't have been too bad overall, since pronghorns prospered into the teeming millions.

A few thousand years ago, however, a new and far more dangerous predator trudged across the Bering land bridge from Asia and discovered pronghorn meat to be rather tasty. The early interaction between Native Americans and antelope was never recorded, of course, but it's likely that these primitive peoples availed themselves of every opportunity to put pronghorn on the menu. The trouble was that getting close enough to an antelope to kill it proved a rather formidable task for a hunter on foot armed with stone-age weapons. Later, after departing Spanish explorers gave Native Americans the great gift of the horse, the hunting probably got a lot better, but even then antelope more than held their own.

One technique of the Native American hunter was simply to park himself with bow and arrow in hand near a

Pronghorn buck in sunlight

water hole visited by antelope. If the animals showed up, if they came close enough, if they didn't spook at his presence, if he got a shot, and if his aim held true, then hunting was good. Until just a few decades ago (and who knows, maybe even today), you could still find here and there on the prairie the remnants of the rock blinds these hunters built near watering places.

But slaying antelope one at a time near water holes is a pretty iffy proposition, especially when hunting is how you plan to feed your family. Consequently, Native Americans developed other techniques for harvesting the fleet and skittish pronghorn, the most successful of which involved considerable teamwork. For several years in the 1830s, former Army officer Benjamin Bonneville led a fur-trading expedition into the American West, making a wealth of observations about the then unexplored land and its people. The following (from Washington Irving's *The Adventures of Captain Bonneville*) is Bonneville's description of a pronghorn-hunting technique employed by a tribe he called the Root Diggers:

> *The women go into the thickest fields of wormwood, and pulling it up in great quantities, construct with it a hedge, about three feet high, inclosing about a hundred acres. A single opening is left for the admission of game. This done, the women conceal themselves behind the wormwood, and wait patiently for the coming of the antelopes, which sometimes enter this spacious trap in considerable numbers. As soon as they are in, the women give the signal, and the men hasten to play their part. But one of them enters the pen at a time; and, after chasing the terrified animals around the enclosure, is relieved by one of his companions. In this way the hunters take their turns, relieving each other, and keeping up a continued pursuit by relays, without fatigue to themselves. The poor antelopes, in the end, are so wearied down, that the whole party of men enter and dispatch them with clubs; not one escaping that has entered the enclosure. The most curious circumstance in this chase is that an animal so fleet and agile as the antelope, and straining for its life, should range round and round this fated enclosure, without attempting to overleap the low barrier which surrounds it. Such, however, is said to be the fact; and such their only mode of hunting the antelope.*

Apparently, Lewis and Clark also were aware of this kind of hunting technique, as they named one small North Dakota stream Goat Pen Creek because of the antelope enclosure Native American hunters had built near its mouth. Also, the Ute and Shoshoni tribes reportedly assembled their people annually for a great pronghorn drive that, if successful, would provide meat for many weeks to come. And on October 16, 1804, Sergeant John Ordway of the Lewis and Clark party recorded the following observation (also in what is now North Dakota):

we Saw a Great nomber of Indians on each side of the River. they were Shooting a flock of Goats [pronghorns] which they had drove into the River. They Shot upwards of 40 of them and got them to Shore. they had Shot them all with their Bows & arrows. we Saw Some of the Goats floating down with the arrows Sticking up in them. we Saw a large flock of Goats back on the hills. which we Suppose they had Scared from the River. our hunter killed 3 Goats out of the Same flock the Indians killed theirs. when the Indians killed the Goats in the River they Swam in & drew them out to each Shore.

Oncc the pioneers came to the West, pronghorn hunting changed radically. Subsistence hunting took on new meaning with the advent of accurate rifles and convenient ammunition. Hordes of hunting settlers replaced the relative handful of Native Americans. Market shooters, who killed whatever they wanted whenever they wanted, hauled off pronghorn carcasses by the wagonload. Antelope—like the bison, the land, the water, and all other resources of nineteenth-century America—seemed infinite, and no one hesitated to exploit or waste whatever they encountered. The notions that hunting needed to be regulated and that wildlife needed to be managed were still many years in the future. So, in just a few decades, pronghorns plummeted from incredible abundance to near extinction.

Professional pronghorn management began in the 1880s with various state laws designed to stem the drastic decline in antelope numbers. It took decades, however, for some of these regulations to really take hold and for states to get serious about managing antelope. Hunting bans, which proliferated around the turn of the century, were easy. Other techniques—such as moving antelope to new areas, discouraging sodbusting, protecting and acquiring habitat, and securing landowner cooperation—were not. In the end, of course, antelope were saved from extinction and began what turned out to be a fantastic comeback (a topic covered in more detail in chapter 2).

As their populations grew during the 1920s and 1930s, pronghorns returned to more and more of their former range, including some areas that had not seen antelope for decades. Often, however, the expansion was slow and

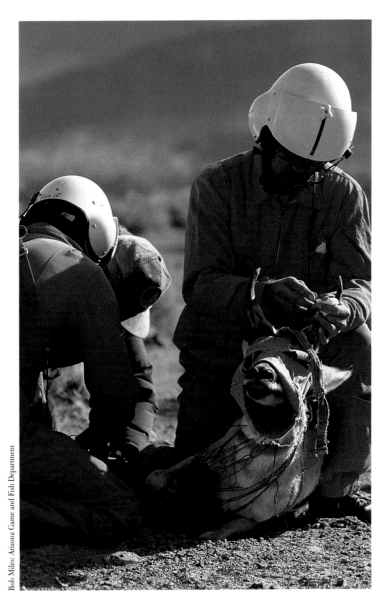

Bob Miles: Arizona Game and Fish Department

Arizona Game and Fish Department relocating pronghorn buck

hindered by the animals' inability or unwillingness to bypass towns, cross waterways, or simply travel through poor habitat to get to good prairie farther on. At the same time, some antelope-rich areas were becoming so densely populated that the harvesting of does might soon become necessary, which seemed a shame when so many other suitable areas had room for additional antelope.

Some wildlife agencies tried capturing newborn fawns, rearing them in captivity, then releasing the young adults in antelope-poor regions. Occasionally, with luck, authorities even managed to capture an adult or two. But these techniques were expensive, time consuming, and not particularly efficient. What pronghorn management needed was a way to move entire bands of adult antelope all at once, but no one really knew if that was possible.

The job of finding out fell to a wildlife biologist named T. Paul Russell, who worked for the New Mexico Department of Game and Fish. Russell thought about this problem a lot, and in 1936 he was ready to take a shot at solving it. Careful scouting had revealed an area where a natural antelope escape route paralleled a fence for a half mile and where the topography was right for concealing an enclosure. Under Russell's supervision, workers set up a temporary wing fence paralleling the existing ranch fence and built a holding pen in a shallow depression at one end of this chute. Their hope was that the antelope, when chased, would run down the fenced chute and into the pen before they realized they were being duped.

One day in December all was ready. Cars and horsemen would haze the antelope into the entrance of the chute, and a hidden man would tug on a long rope to close the pen gate as soon as the animals were inside. The pronghorns cooperated, and soon thirty-five antelope were galloping down the channel. The leaders raced on into the enclosure, but before the entire herd could get inside, the first arrivals realized their mistake and thundered back out again. In the melee, the gate never got closed, and so thirty-five terrified antelope were now charging back up the chute. Cars, horses, and men on foot attempted to block their path, but to little avail. In a dusty donnybrook of confusion, the antelope dodged their pursuers and surged on past to freedom. "The score," wrote Russell, "was several bruised antelope, including one that ran into a car; a man knocked down by the momentum of an antelope; a big buck roped by [one of the workers]; and some valuable experience."

The key revelation in that experience was to have a gate on the chute some distance upstream from the holding pen. By closing this gate as soon as the pronghorns had passed, the animals could still be contained even if they did not immediately enter the holding pen. They could always be hazed into the pen later.

So it was that on the morning of April 5, 1937, twenty-nine pronghorns found themselves contained in a rudimentary enclosure on the New Mexico plains. Before sundown that day, they were free again on new habitat miles away. Soon, other states got into the antelope-capturing act, releasing starter squads of pronghorns in piece after piece of available habitat. Airplanes—and later helicopters—often replaced horses and cars for herding the antelope, and a few other details also underwent refinement, but Russell's technique became the model for capturing America's swiftest mammal. Today, pronghorn relocation is a common tool of wildlife managers.

Although pronghorns have proven eminently amenable to transplantation, mistakes have occurred. The first was in Florida. In the 1960s, W. Tom McBroom, then a game commissioner in Florida's fourth district, took a real liking to the pronghorns he enjoyed hunting in Colorado. After several years of campaigning, McBroom finally convinced enough of the right people that Florida should have its own antelope herd, and so in January 1966 authorities built an elaborate antelope trap on a large ranch near Colorado Springs, Colorado. Workers herded a few dozen prong-horns into the enclosure and, after appropriate periods to allow the animals to quiet down, boxed thirty-eight of them in plywood crates. Trucks ferried the antelope to the Colorado Springs airport, where an Eastern Airlines plane and crew stood ready to speed the animals on to Florida.

Five hours later, the plane touched down in Orlando, and after another truck ride the antelope immigrants arrived at their final destination, a large ranch in the Kissimmee Valley. Jim Powell, formerly a biologist with the Florida Game and Freshwater Fish Commission, recalls succinctly what happened then: "Those antelope came ten feet out of their crates, saw more water than they knew existed, and were never heard from again. They were about as suitable for Florida as polar bears." The head of one of those pronghorns later turned up in a taxidermist's shop, but the rest of them did indeed vanish.

A more fruitful, but also ultimately unsuccessful, reloca-tion occurred in Hawaii in 1959. In December of that year,

seven adult does and thirty-one fawns made the long journey from the mainland to Lanai, a volcanic island of 140 square miles about fifty miles southeast of Oahu. Six weeks later, the herd had dwindled to eighteen animals, but those sur-vivors held on, and by 1966 there were more than two hundred pronghorns on the island. Officials authorized a limited number of hunting permits, and in August of that year Hawaiian sportsmen took thirty-three pronghorns. Then something (unrelated to the hunting) went wrong, and the census began to drop. In 1971, fewer than seventy antelope remained, and a year later there were only thirty. Before long, the last Hawaiian pronghorn had disappeared.

Although the reasons for this herd's demise are open to speculation, at least one biologist who studied the situation pinpointed plant succession as the culprit. For half a century prior to the pronghorn introduction, cattle had grazed (and overgrazed) Lanai, giving parts of the island the look of Wyoming. Then the cattle were removed and the antelope brought in. But the pronghorns, with their relatively mini-mal dietary requirements, could not keep up with the bountiful plant growth that followed the bovines' removal. Thick brush, clearly unsuitable pronghorn habitat, spread over much of the island, and inedible or less nutritious plants replaced good forage. Does began producing fewer fawns, and before long the entire project petered out.

One relocation that could have worked but didn't occurred in Washington, the only western state with no historical record of pronghorn residency. In 1940, authorities released in the south-central part of that state thirty-eight adult antelope, graduates of a program of bottle-feeding fawns captured in Nevada and Oregon. By 1950, this herd had increased to one hundred animals, ten of which were then moved to an area near the town of Ritzville. Six years later, these pronghorns had multiplied to eighty animals, and it appeared that Washington was well on its way to having two thriving antelope populations. Between 1970 and 1975, however, both groups died out—for reasons that are still not well understood. Another relocation effort in 1968, involving twenty-two antelope from Oregon, ended the same way, with the last of those animals perishing by 1980.

Dead-end relocations like these notwithstanding, pronghorn management has been a colossal success. Today, the pronghorn species that in the 1920s numbered ten or fifteen thousand stands at about a million strong.

Shoulder mount of pronghorn buck, Taos, New Mexico

It is no secret, of course, that the amazing comeback of the seemingly doomed pronghorn occurred because of this animal's status as a prized game animal. It was hunters (among others) who pushed for closed seasons, bag limits, and other protective regulations. And it was hunters who footed many of the bills for pronghorn restoration. Few groups in history have ever petitioned their governments to increase their taxes, but in the 1930s America's sport hunters did just that.

Left to their own devices, state wildlife agencies simply did not have the wherewithal to properly protect and enhance the populations of wild animals that had for decades been either exploited or ignored. With wildlife habitat disappearing from the plains in great clouds of dust and species after species languishing for lack of management funds, sportsmen in the 1930s lobbied for a federal tax on firearms and ammunition, with the revenue to be returned to the states for wildlife management. Hunters were most interested in game animals like antelope, elk, deer, and waterfowl, but dozens of nongame species also stood to benefit. In 1937, President Franklin D. Roosevelt signed the Pittman-Robertson Federal Aid In Wildlife Restoration Act into law.

For the first time, state agencies could afford to census their wildlife populations, protect habitat, study species, restock areas with transplanted animals, conduct research, and in other ways help the wild nations. The Pittman-Robertson Act currently levies an 11 percent excise tax on sporting arms and ammunition and a 10 percent tax on handguns and archery equipment. These self-induced taxes annually bring in nearly 150 million dollars—a whopping 2 billion dollars to date. Lots of species benefited (and continue to benefit) from the Pittman-Robertson Act and the conservation ethic born around the turn of the century, but none more so than the pronghorn.

The result has been, since the 1940s, a great upsurge in the sport hunting of pronghorns. Early in this century, no state permitted pronghorn hunting. By 1934, populations had rebounded sufficiently to allow open seasons in only three states (harvesting about two thousand animals). By the 1960s, the hunting of pronghorns was allowed in fourteen states, and today fifteen states (all those in the West except Oklahoma and Washington) plus Alberta and Saskatchewan in Canada allow pronghorn hunting. Wyoming hunters take the most antelope, about 63,000 in 1993, and Montana is next with a 1993 harvest of 43,000 pronghorns.

With most major predators now absent from the plains, sport hunting has become the wildlife manager's primary tool for controlling pronghorn populations. Without hunting, antelope might in many places overrun the available habitat, eat themselves into starvation, and make enemies of every rancher in sight. Of course, hunting also provides untallied days of recreation for thousands of people and puts a lot of meat on a lot of tables, although an average antelope does not exactly fill up the freezer with its twenty-five or thirty pounds of meat (excluding the bones).

Many of today's antelope hunters, however, are as much in pursuit of trophies as table fare. The pronghorn is one of the few species to offer the average hunter a reasonable expectation of shooting an animal with respectable horns. The open terrain provides a degree of accessibility not possible with elk, mountain goats, bighorn sheep or (in many cases) even deer, and it is generally accepted that taking a "nice" pronghorn requires fewer hunting skills than shooting a comparably antlered or horned member of those other species. Among hunters, 12-inch horns (measured from skull to tip over the longest route) are considered poor, 13-inchers are fair, 14+ is good, 15+ is excellent, and anything over 16 inches is very rare and remarkable. The all-time largest horns are just over twenty inches. With its strikingly colored coat, a pronghorn makes a very attractive wall mount.

One final note: Antelope hunting is not for everybody. Some people quite understandably have no desire to shoot an antelope. Such nonhunters sometimes have a difficult time understanding how anyone else could choose to kill so beautiful an animal. Whole volumes have been penned to explain the hunting instinct and heritage, so it would be pointless to attempt to fully address that issue here. One point that often gets lost in such discussions, however, is the relationship between an individual animal and the entire species. Everything in nature is geared toward the preservation of the species, often at the expense of the individual. Hunting works this way, too. Being shot is, of course, the worst possible thing for any given antelope, but killing some pronghorns is precisely what allows others to live and the species to survive. Most hunters care very much about the preservation of the species they hunt. They contribute a lot of money—and often time and talent as well—to ensure that our wildlife resources will be around for a long time to come. Hunters are one of the main reasons why the white and rusty-brown antelope remains the dominant living symbol of the North American prairie.

The Other Antelope

MORE THAN ONE KIND of pronghorn graces the western plains. Back when all the newly discovered North American animals were getting their official Latin names, biologists often quarreled over the precise differences that distinguished one creature from another. Telling a marmot from a magpie was easy, but in many other cases animals in one region differed only slightly from animals in another. Some experts looked at the whole creature, kicked their common sense into overdrive, and decreed that if two animals were for all intents and purposes the same, they should have the same name despite minor differences in size, shape,

or other features. These folks were called lumpers, because they liked to lump closely related animals together.

Other experts, however, were splitters, folks who looked not at how much alike two animals were, but rather at the small differences that separated them. The two groups often engaged in lengthy debate about just how different similar animals had to be before they got separate names. If lumpers carried the day, a group of animals with slight physical distinctions would all have the same name. If splitters prevailed, the creatures got different names, usually expressed in terms of subspecies

Sonoran pronghorn, Cabeza Prieta Wildlife Refuge, Arizona

(Photograph by James Tallon)

(also called races). The splitters did a pretty good job on pronghorns.

In 1818, zoologist George Ord named the pronghorn *Antilocapra americana* (which means American goat-antelope), but it wasn't long before people (usually biologists with microscopes and close-measuring calipers) began noting slight differences among pronghorns from different parts of the country. Eventually, the list of documented subspecies looked like this:

> *Antilocapra americana americana* (common pronghorn)
> *Antilocapra americana mexicana* (Mexican pronghorn)
> *Antilocapra americana oregona* (Oregon pronghorn)
> *Antilocapra americana peninsularis* (peninsular pronghorn)
> *Antilocapra americana sonoriensis* (Sonoran pronghorn)

From a layperson's point of view, these are all the same animals, although one may have a slightly smaller skull, another moderately darker hair, and so on. Take five individuals of each race and run them together to create a herd of twenty-five, and the odds are good that no civilian could ever separate them again. In fact, it might take some mighty sharp biologists and plenty of DNA testing to unscramble the herd. Confusing things even further, antelope of the *americana* race (the garden variety pronghorn) have on sev-

eral occasions been released in areas where they might interbreed with one or another of the other subspecies. So, bearing in mind that the physical differences among these groups are slight and that the distinctions in some cases might be blurred by blended genetics, here's a brief synopsis of the pronghorn clan:

ANTILOCAPRA AMERICANA AMERICANA (common pronghorn)

This is the parent species, the mother of all American antelope, so to speak. These are the animals you see on the prairies of Wyoming, Montana, South Dakota, and nearly everywhere else antelope roam. Most of the information in this book applies to these animals.

ANTILOCAPRA AMERICANA MEXICANA (Mexican pronghorn)

The Mexican pronghorn (also called the Chihuahuan pronghorn) historically existed in southeast Arizona, Mexico, and parts of Texas and New Mexico. New Mexico still has a small uncensused herd in the southwestern part of the state. In Texas, this race consists solely of a small (also untallied) population near the town of Marathon in Brewster County. For most management purposes, they are not distinguished from *americana* pronghorns, but Texas authorities are careful not to introduce other antelope into this region, because the resulting crossbreeding would likely destroy the purity of the mexicana gene pool.

This race disappeared from Arizona about 1920, primarily due to uncontrolled subsistence hunting and changing land-use patterns. In the 1980s, biologists moved about four hundred Chihuahuan pronghorns from Texas to five sites in Arizona, mostly in the central part of the state. Three of these groups are doing well, with mexicana pronghorns now numbering about five hundred. The outlook is not particularly promising, however, due to the loss of habitat as central Arizona undergoes development.

Only very subtle physical distinctions set the Chihuahuan race apart from its sister subspecies—color of horn, slightly smaller body size, and skull measurements. As far as habitat is concerned, this animal lies midway between the desert-dwelling Sonoran and the common americana subspecies that thrives on the relatively wet prairies of most western states. The Chihuahuan seems best adapted to areas where summer monsoons deliver twelve to fifteen inches of rain.

ANTILOCAPRA AMERICANA OREGONA (Oregon pronghorn)

This race is said to live on the shrub and grassland steppes of southeastern Oregon and adjacent states, but many experts say these animals exist mostly in the minds of a few of the splitters mentioned above. Oregon pronghorns became a subspecies in 1932, primarily on the basis of their slightly larger bodies, feet, and horns. They also are a little paler in color and have a bit less black on the face and mane. The specimens used to name this race came from the Hart Mountain area of southern Oregon, a population that may extend into adjoining rangelands in California and Nevada, where they could easily interbreed with the americana race. In fact, recent DNA tests could not distinguish between these two. Consequently, there is a growing scientific consensus that no such animal as Antilocapra americana oregona exists.

ANTILOCAPRA AMERICANA PENINSULARIS (peninsular pronghorn)

All that remains of this race are about 100 to 250 animals in the Vizcaíno Desert of central Baja California in Mexico, a figure that is up appreciably from the 50 or so animals that existed a decade ago. Though never very numerous, peninsular pronghorns did at one time occupy much more of this peninsula than the twelve hundred or so square miles that constitutes their current range. They also existed in parts of southern California. The reasons for their decline mirror those for the decline of the other desert subspecies.

Like the Sonorans, these animals also may exist without free water to drink, getting what little moisture they need from infrequent rains, plants, and dew that collects on vegetation courtesy of ocean fogs that drift inland. Peninsular pronghorns have darker colors than their kin and characteristic blackish tips on their ears. There also are minor differences of horns and teeth. This race will probably never become plentiful, but if a proposed relocation to southern California occurs, numbers could rise somewhat.

ANTILOCAPRA AMERICANA SONORIENSIS (Sonoran pronghorn)

The Sonoran pronghorn once roamed the arid Southwest from near Phoenix and Tucson in the east, across the Colorado River into California, and south into Mexico. It's impossible to know how many once existed, since they likely mingled with other races in parts of their range. Suffice it to say that once there were many more than the approximately five hundred that remain today. Authorities used to think that over-hunting was the primary cause of the Sonoran's decline, but decades of complete protection have not increased the population greatly. Consequently, current thinking points the finger of blame at habitat loss due to livestock overgrazing and the dewatering of some major rivers in the region.

So isolated were these animals on such forbidding terrain that only in 1945 were they "discovered" by taxonomists, when a researcher happened to examine closely two skulls and a skin collected in 1932. Generally, Sonoran pronghorns are distinguished from their kin by their slightly smaller stature, slightly lighter color, and some minimal differences in cranial measurements.

The Sonoran's main claim to fame is its incredible ability to exist at all in one of the hottest, driest regions on earth. That these animals can live where they do seems something of a miracle. Their preferred habitat consists mostly of flat, sandy, rocky desert, where creosote, palo verde, and cactus are the primary vegetation. Rainfall is scant, sporadic, and in some places in some years non-existent. Daytime temperatures sometimes hit 120 degrees Fahrenheit. There are no towns, no ranches, no mines. Just desert and a few hardy Sonoran pronghorns. These animals are so adapted to their harsh environment that they may have evolved an entirely waterless lifestyle. Biologists aren't ready to say for sure, but Sonorans could be getting by without ever drinking water. With surface water a real rarity, they appear to get most and possibly all their moisture from the vegetation they eat and by licking droplets of dew.

In 1970, the U.S. federal government declared this race an endangered (sub)species. Luckily, the few surviving

Sonorans have chosen to live on public lands—the Cabeza Prieta National Wildlife Refuge, Organ Pipe Cactus National Monument, and an Air Force gunnery range, all in Arizona. They currently number about 250. Approximately that many more are believed to exist in Mexico (where they receive considerably less protection than in this country).

The future of the Sonoran pronghorn is an open question. With so few of the animals in existence, they certainly must be considered one of America's most imperiled species. On the other hand, their habitat remains relatively secure, and their numbers have been slowly increasing. Proposals have been put forth to create new herds of Sonorans and to breed them in captivity, but so far none of this has come to fruition. In the meantime, these desert dwellers will likely continue eking out a living from some of the harshest, most inhospitable habitat on earth.

For most intents and purposes, there is only one pronghorn, and that animal remains rather abundant on the vast western plains. Whether the other members of the clan survive far into the future is important, sure, but not crucial. America's antelope have already passed the great survivability test and should be around for a long time to come.

Pronghorn buck standing on Wyoming road

Afterword

ONE DAY NOT TOO long ago, I tired of the ceaseless plodding that often defines my antelope hunting forays and chose to park myself in a tiny weathered depression just below the top of a little ridge. Well hidden from prying eyes, I thought perhaps an antelope might come within rifle range of me instead of the other way around. That didn't happen, but something else did.

The view was panoramic, and it wasn't long before I started to see pronghorns. A little band crossed from left to right half a mile away. Before long, a small herd passed through headed in the opposite direction. Every so often, a single doe or a doe with fawns traipsed by on their hurried

ways to somewhere else. When the sun shone just right, I could in the far-off distance detect the white-rumped presence of two more sizable antelope aggregations. Sweeping the countryside slowly with my binoculars revealed still more pronghorns—here a reclining pair, there a few grazers, and elsewhere a decent buck bedded wisely and unstalkably on a little knoll.

Quite simply, the antelope were everywhere, and I was astonished that such abundance could grow from such seemingly desolate land. Knowing the history of these creatures, I marveled, too, at what seemed to be their complete repopulating of habitat that had at one time stood entirely

Pronghorn does at sunset

(Photograph by Robert Winslow)

131

empty of antelope. Had my grandfather sat in this spot on an October day seventy years ago, he likely would have seen no antelope—or at most one or two. And now I beheld them in every direction.

It would be easy to become complacent about antelope, to see them as indestructible prairie icons that will endure forever. The other great beasts have all been eliminated from the plains. Bison live today at human pleasure only in tiny selected fragments of their former domain. Grizzlies and elk were long ago driven to mountain hideouts where dense forests offer concealment and sanctuary. The gray wolf fled to Canada and only now is making a tentative return to this country. But the pronghorn remains, standing tall and bountiful as the preeminent species on the vast western flatland. Pronghorns took the best shot a destructive human society could deliver and bounced back to reclaim nearly all of their former range. Long before humans arrived here, pronghorns graced this continent's plains. Might they not postdate us as well?

Perhaps. But not without help. Like it or not, the human species has the awesome power to irrevocably alter ancient natural systems, to change the face of the planet, and to extinguish virtually any life form. Were it to become the human desire, pronghorns could be made as extinct as

dodo birds, or confined to a handful of paltry pastures in the nation's parks or reduced like the California condor to a few incarcerated individuals. God may have given us the pronghorn, but people can take it away.

Such a dark day, however, is far from imminent. The American antelope remains the symbol of wildlife success, not failure. Like the Phoenix, the mythical Egyptian bird that rose anew from its own ashes, pronghorns also have been reborn, have been given a second chance. Their recovery from the brink of extinction—hailed by some as the greatest comeback in wildlife history—did not happen in a vacuum. It happened because the right people did the right things at the right times. Likewise, pronghorns continue to prosper because a complex network of conservationists, landowners, hunters, wildlife enthusiasts, and professional game managers want them to.

And so it will go. As long as people value antelope—and grizzly bears, elk, black-footed ferrets, wolves, and all the rest—we will have them with us to enjoy. But it would be a mistake to believe that any wild creature is forever. The wildlife annuls are littered with the names of species that no longer exist. Once, pronghorns came close to joining that rueful roster, and once is enough.

Further Reading

Ahlstrom, Mark. *The Pronghorn*. Mankato, Minnesota: Crestwood House, 1986. (For young readers.)

Bere, Rennie. *Antelopes*. New York: Arco Publishing, 1970.

Caton, John. *The Antelope and Deer of America*. New York: Forest and Stream Publishing, 1877.

Einarsen, Arthur. *The Pronghorn Antelope and Its Management*. Washington D. C.: The Wildlife Management Institute, 1948.

Popowski, Bert, and Wilf Pyle. *The Hunter's Book of the Pronghorn Antelope*. Tulsa, Oklahoma: Winchester Press, 1982.

Van Wormer, Joe. *The World of the Pronghorn*. New York: J.B. Lippincott, 1969.

Index

About the Author and Photographers

GARY TURBAK, a native of South Dakota, is a full-time freelance writer who authored Northland's *Survivors in the Shadows, Twilight Hunters*, the Survivors Series for Children, and articles in many widely circulated periodicals. Gary has won many awards for his environmental and natural history articles and essays. He is a Vietnam veteran, a cat lover, a former teacher, a professional photographer, and a lifelong student of wildlife. Gary and his wife, Jan, live in Missoula, Montana.

ALAN and SANDY CAREY are a professional wildlife photography team whose work has appeared in such publications as *National Geographic, Life,* and *Time,* as well as the Northland books *Among the Elk, In the Path of the Grizzly,* and *Twilight Hunters*. Their love of wildlife and the desire to photograph animals and birds in their natural habitats has taken Alan, Sandy, and their five-year-old daughter, Christina, to many parts of the world.